SERVICENOW DEVELOPMENT HANDBOOK

A compendium of pro-tips, guidelines, and best practices for ServiceNow developers

Tim Woodruff

To Ciel, Roger, Genie, Chuck, Kim, and Seven

Special thanks to technical and content editors
Ashley Snyder
Kevin Eldridge
John Helebrant
Maria Gabriela Ochoa Perez
Matt Hernandez
JarodM

And thanks to the readers who wrote in to contribute

Version 1.4

This compendium will be updated more often than a typical book. Minor-to-medium content updates and additions will be made within this edition, and major updates will come in the next edition.
The changelog can be found at
http://changelog.sngeek.com/.

If you've purchased this book on Kindle, you can check for updates and ensure that you have the latest version of this edition for free by going to http://update.sngeek.com/.

If you've purchased this book on paperback, you may purchase the Kindle edition for only $2.99 at
http://kindlehandbook.sngeek.com/.

CONTENTS

ABOUT THE AUTHOR

TIM WOODRUFF has worked in IT for over a decade and has been writing software for even longer. For the past several years though, Tim has narrowed his focus (for the most part) to ServiceNow's IT Service Management platform, otherwise known as the "Now" platform. He continues to work with several companies as an independent consultant to help implement and manage ServiceNow instances.

Tim has written multiple books on ServiceNow's Now platform (which you can find at http://books.sngeek.com/), and writes a ServiceNow development blog as time permits, that's full of tips, tricks, best-practices, and free ServiceNow tools (http://snprotips.com/).

You might say Tim is a huge nerd; he enjoys reading sci-fi and non-fiction, as well as listening to audiobooks, studying physics and programming, debating philosophy, exploring ghost towns, and long road-trip adventures.

You can find Tim on LinkedIn at https://www.linkedin.com/in/sn-timw/, or on Twitter at @TheTimWoodruff.

INTRODUCTION

BEING A SERVICENOW ARCHITECT with a technical training background, I often find myself teaching development and administration standards and best-practices in ServiceNow, as well as why the best-practices are important. Having a complete understanding of why a given standard is what it is (and why it's important), will not only make people more likely to adhere to it, but will empower them to apply the underlying concepts to other areas and make them more effective administrators, developers, or architects. That's the spirit in which this developer handbook was written: A spirit of teaching and explaining, not simply listing out a series of edicts under the heading of "best-practice".

Keep in mind that these are **guidelines**. For every rule in this compendium, there is probably at least one exception. What's important, is understanding when you're deviating from the best-practice guidelines, and having a good reason for it. Better yet, documenting that reason so any developers who come after you won't have to guess! For example, the standards make it clear that DOM (Document Object Model) manipulation is not ideal, because it is not well supported and may result in issues as ServiceNow changes the way pages are rendered in the platform. A good example of this issue is the Service Portal, which recently broke most, if not all DOM access.

However, there are some cases where you've tried all the alternatives you could think of and couldn't find a better way to accomplish some business-critical change. In these cases, it is always wise to reach out to your architect team first (if you have one) or fellow developers, to see if there might be a better way that you can come up with together. However, sometimes a better way cannot be found. This is okay! Just remember to document that you tried, and to have (and document) a good reason for doing things in a non-standard way.

This is a condensed "developer guide", not a complete ServiceNow training course in book-form. It assumes that you've already become at least somewhat familiar with the ServiceNow platform, and that you already have at least a working knowledge of JavaScript.

If you don't yet feel comfortable calling yourself a "ServiceNow developer", consider reading another of my books to get up to speed: **Learning ServiceNow** (ISBN-13: 978-1785883323) which you can find at the URL http://books.sngeek.com/. As long as you have a basic understanding of the ServiceNow platform though, think of this book as your roadmap to ensuring that your work in ServiceNow will be clean, effective, safe, and robust.

***Note:** If you find any errors or omissions in this book, please get in touch with me! You can reach me any time via Twitter at @TheTimWoodruff.*

NAMING CONVENTIONS

How to be kind to your future self

*There are only two hard things in Computer
Science: cache invalidation and naming things.*
—Phil Karlton

What the heck does "inBusStNasS" mean!?
—Me, all the time

Whether it's a variable, a field, a parameter, a descriptor, a table, or anything else – names and labels matter! With the exception of variable names like **theValueOfTheFieldUsedForDeterminingIfARecordIsActiveOrNot**, more descriptive field names are generally preferred. Imagine if that variable were instead called FldValActvDet. Without context, you'd have a heck of a time figuring out what sort of data it might contain!

The most important thing about naming conventions, is that they make sense. If you're not certain about what to do, or not confident of the best solution, ask your team! Your company or client might have an existing standard around naming conventions; and if not, creating one is a great way to show initiative! Taking a little responsibility for maintaining the quality of your instance is a great way to build a name for yourself within your organization and get a career boost because of it!

TABLES

One of the most commonly neglected conventions around table naming, is to always give your table a **singular** name. **Fields** can have plural names if they can hold multiple values, but tables should always have a singular name. This applies to both the **name**, and the **label** of a table.

Consider some of the core ITIL tables: *incident*, *sc_cat_item*, *problem*, and *change*. These tables all have singular names. They are not named "incidents", or "problems", for example. In the table's dictionary record, there will be a place to enter the pluralized version of the table label, which can be used to describe multiple records in that table. The system will default to the table's label followed by an "s". However, if you have a table labeled something like **Logbook Entry** [u_logbook_entry], the system might pluralize it as **Logbook Entrys**, which is not the correct spelling. In this case, you would have to update the plural label to **Logbook Entries**, but the label would remain singular.

Note: The latest versions of ServiceNow seems to do a little better with correctly pluralizing most words in table names for the pluralized labels but be sure to double-check!

There are a few OOB table names that defy this rule, but that doesn't mean that we should emulate this mistake! For example, the **System Properties** [sys_properties] table is pluralized. This is a remnant of very old versions of ServiceNow, and since table names are very difficult to change without major system-wide impacts, it has remained plural.

Another good general for table naming conventions, is to follow a separate convention when naming certain specialized types of tables. For example, **data lookup** tables are tables which define the relationship between selections in certain fields in a given record, in order to facilitate some business logic. A data lookup table might therefore contain a set of fields and corresponding values that, when found on a **task** record, should result in assignment to a specific group, or the record being set to a specific priority. When creating a data lookup table, it's not a bad idea to begin the table name with **u_dl**. You can create new Data Lookup Definitions from the **System Policy > Rules > Data Lookup Definitions** module in the Application Navigator.

*Note: In order to automatically apply certain business logic, your custom data lookup table must extend the **Data Lookup Matcher Rules** [dl_matcher] table. You may need to enable the **Data Lookup and Record Matching Support** table to enable this.*

Similarly, **many-to-many** tables should usually have a name beginning with **u_m2m**. These naming conventions are less *friendly* than for normal tables, but they help to make it clear when you're working with tables that serve a specific utilitarian function. For example, **dl_matcher_incident_priority** makes it clear that we're dealing with a utility table, whereas a name like **incident_priority** would be much less clear (Is this a list of Incident priorities?)

FIELD NAMES AND LABELS

In general, names should reflect labels and vice-versa. If you have a field labeled **Business Justification**, it should not be named "u_string_3", nor "u_ncc_ad_string", nor even the less-unacceptable "u_bus_jus". Unless the label needs to be quite long for some reason (in which case you might want to reach out to other team members or an architect for advice), it usually makes sense to have the name match. In this case: **u_business_justification**.

Also remember that it's not necessary to include the table name in your field labels or names. For example, the **Number** field on the Incident table is not named **incident_number**, or labeled **Incident Number**. It's just **Number**. This is because it's clear that it's the Incident number, given that it's on the Incident table. If it were a reference to a different table, a name indicating the table it references might be more appropriate. For example, a field on the Incident table which references the Problem table might appropriately be called **Related Problem** with the name **u_related_problem**. However, if it's a field that might need to be changed to reference a different or more base table in the future, you might leave the **name** (which is difficult to change) vague, but have the **label** be **Related Problem**.

In the same vein, it is usually unnecessary to add "ID" or "number" (as just a couple of examples) to a field name or label. For example, if you have a field which references the Incident table, where the display value is the **Number** field, you do not need to name the field **Incident Number**, or **Incident ID**. Simply **Incident** is sufficient for a label and is recommended. It will contain the number as the display value, sure, but it'll also contain a reference to the entire record which allows you to view all of the other details as well. In a sense, the field wouldn't contain the Incident number, it would contain the entire Incident (or at least, a reference to the entire Incident).

VARIABLES

*Note: This section only refers to **JavaScript** variables, not **catalog** variables.*

JavaScript variables that point to **functions**, **objects**, and **primitives** should be in **camelCase**. **Class** names on the other hand, should be in **TitleCase**. All variable names should start with a letter (a lower-case letter, in the case of non-class variables). Finally, Constants should be in all-uppercase. For example:

```
var MYCUSTOMTABLEQUERY = 'u_active=true^sys_updated_onONLast
30
days@javascript:gs.beginningOfLast30Days()@javascript:gs.endO
fLast30Days()';
```

Note: JS doesn't technically have "classes" per se, but we implement them on the ServiceNow server-side using Script Includes so for those, we use TitleCase.

The following example script contains multiple examples of various variable types, and best-practice naming conventions for them.

```
var assigneeSysID = getAssigneeSysID('Johnny B Developer');

function getAssigneeSysID(assigneeName) {
    var assigneeUtils;
    gs.debug('Got argument: "' + arg + '".',
'exampleArgument'); //todo: Remove this after testing, to
avoid unnecessary production logs
    var grUser = new GlideRecord('sys_user');
    //If user is found
    if (grUser.get('name', assigneeName)) {
        assigneeUtils = new AssigneeUtils();
        //Check if the user is a valid assignee. If so,
return the user's sys_id.
        //Otherwise, fall out of conditional blocks
        if (assigneeUtils.checkIfValidAssignee(grUser)) {
            return grUser.getUniqueValue();
        }
    }
    //If user cannot be found, or the user is not a
    // valid assignee, fall through to return false

    return false;
}
```

Another good rule of thumb when it comes to variable declaration, is to never declare variables inside of loop initializations (like `while` or `for` loops). This would lead to them being re-initialized on every loop! It's also not a good idea because if that loop never fires, then the variable is never initialized; so, if it were used outside of the loop, it would be undefined and may result in an error. Also, if you had a **nested** loop that used the same iterator, you would get very surprising behavior indeed; possibly even resulting in an infinite loop.

It's also not a good idea to declare a variable inside a conditional or loop code-block (`if`/`while`/`for`) like so:

```
var i = 12;
while (i < 10) {
    var howMany = i + 42;
    i++;
}
console.log(howMany); //undefined!
```

This is for several reasons, not least of which is that if the loop or conditional block doesn't run for some reason, accessing it outside of that block could result in an error that could be exposed to the user if un-caught. Instead, declare your variables just above your control and conditional blocks, or maybe even hoist the declaration all the way to the top of the function/scope.

When you initialize a variable, also consider initializing it to a **default** value. For example, integer variables might be initialized to -1 as a default value (unless it might end up being a negative number as part of normal operation) like so:

```
var i = 12,
howMany = 0;

while (i < 10) {
    var howMany = i + 42;
    i++;
}

console.log(howMany);
```

OBJECT PROPERTIES

Object **property names** (also called **Keys**) may contain underscores in lieu of spaces, or they may be declared in camelCase. The important thing is to make sure that your conventions are consistent, at least within any one script.

```
var myObj = {
    property_one: 'This is the first property',
    property_two: 42
};
myObj.property_three = 'This is the third property of myObj';
myObj['property_four'] = true;
```

GLIDERECORDS

GlideRecord variables should begin with `gr`, and should usually indicate the table name, or at least something about the record that is identifiable. GlideRecord variables should also be singular; not plural. It might be tempting to call your variable something like `grReqItems`, but remember that at any given time, that variable only contains a single record's data, and should therefore be singular. **Arrays** however, are often plural. For example:

```
var sectionNames = g_form.getSectionNames();
```

It's alright to just name your GlideRecord variable after the table name (`grIncident`, for example). However, it's also acceptable and not unwise to indicate something about the **query**. For example, you might name your GlideRecord variable `grOpenIncident` to indicate that you're iterating through only Incident records where the **Active** field is set to true. Just remember that if you modify your code and change the query or something else about the variable and need to change its name to match, you must update its name **scope-wide**, so that the variable name always corresponds to its contents. This is *especially* important when you have multiple GlideRecords on a single table. Even if you don't have multiple, it's a good idea to name your GlideRecord variables with more descriptive names. Just remember to keep them singular.

```
var grOpenIncident = new GlideRecord('incident');
grOpenIncident.addActiveQuery(); //Get only open Incidents
grOpenIncident.query();
//etc...
```

ITERATORS

Iterators are similar to normal variables, except that they store some information which relates to the state of the loop in which they're used, and should be used in block-scope only. This means that if you have a `for()` `{}` block, the iterator variable you use should typically only be used inside the curly braces that define the code block that executes for each iteration of that loop.

If you know what sort of things you're iterating through, it's a good idea to use a meaningful name, as you can see in the following example:

```
function Instance(name, url, production) {
    this.name = name;
    this.url = url;
    this.production = production;
}
var myInstances = {
    'dev': new Instance('dev', 'http://sndev.service-
now.com/', false),
    'test': new Instance('test', 'http://sntest.service-
now.com/', false),
    'prod': new Instance('prod', 'http://sn.service-
now.com/', true)
};

var snInstance;
for (snInstance in myInstances) {
    if (myInstances.hasOwnProperty(snInstance) &&
myInstances[snInstance].production === true) {
        console.log('The production instance URL is: ' +
myInstances[snInstance].url);
    }
}
```

In the example above, I knew that I was iterating over an object consisting of ServiceNow **instances**, so I named my iterator variable `snInstance`. However, it's perfectly alright to use something like `prop` or even `p` as an iterator, as you can see here:

```
function Person(firstName, ageInYears, heightInCm, gender) {
    this.firstName = firstName;
    this.ageInYears = ageInYears;
}
function Family(lastName, parents, children) {
    this.lastName = lastName;
    this.parents = parents;
    this.children = children;
}
```

```
var homerSimpson = new Person('Homer', 42);
var margeSimpson = new Person('Marge', 41);
var lisaSimpson = new Person('Lisa', 8);
var bartSimpton = new Person('Bart', 7);
var maggieSimpson = new Person('Maggie', 1);

var theSimpsons = new Family(
    'Simpson',
    [homerSimpson, margeSimpson], //parents
    [lisaSimpson, bartSimpton, maggieSimpson] //children
);

for (var p in theSimpsons) {
    if (theSimpsons.hasOwnProperty(p)) {
        console.log('This property is a(n) ' + typeof
theSimpsons[p]);
    }
}
```

Here, we're iterating over the `theSimpsons` object, which contains a string, and two arrays. Each array then contains multiple `Person` objects. One very important thing to remember about iterators, is that if you have a **nested** loop, you should not use the same iterator name for the nested loop, as you did for the outer loop; otherwise the nested loop will override the value of the outer loop's iterator and could result in an infinite loop!

It is a good idea to avoid doing much heavy-lifting in a nested loop whenever possible. For example, it's not often a good idea to iterate over a GlideRecord inside a `while` loop that's already iterating over *another* GlideRecord. This would result in a separate query for every result in the outer loop! There is usually a better and more efficient way to do this, such as using the first query to populate an array of sys_ids, which can then be used in the query filter for the second lookup. Only use a nested query if you can't come up with a better solution.

When iterating over arrays, you always know that your iterator variable will contain an integer, since arrays do not contain named properties like other types of objects. In this case, as with the `p` iterator for object properties, it's perfectly alright to use an iterator with a name like `i`. You may also choose to use something more descriptive, like `index` or `count`. If you know that your array should contain only a specific type of thing, you may even choose to use a more appropriate name as you can see in the following example:

```
var food;
var favoriteFoods = [
    'non-dairy beef',
```

```
        'evaporated water',
        'raw halibut',
        'banana and pickle sandwiches'
];
var msg = 'I like...';
for (food = 0; food < favoriteFoods.length; food++) {
    if (food > 0) {
            msg += ' and '
    }
            msg += favoriteFoods[food];
    }
console.log(msg + '!');
```

However, the following notation would also have been completely acceptable for the loop above:

```
for (i = 0; i < favoriteFoods.length; i++) {
    if (i > 0) {
            msg += ' and '
    }
    msg += favoriteFoods[i];
}
```

In JavaScript, there are multiple ways to perform a loop in your code. When iterating over the properties of an object, it is common to use syntax similar to the following:

```
var prop;
for (prop in obj) {
    /*code here*/
}
```

This is fine for a start, but remember that whenever you iterate over the properties of an object, you probably don't want to iterate over **non-enumerable** properties, or properties along the inheritance chain, which can result in irretrievable values and undefined/inaccessible property names. To avoid that, whenever iterating over an object, the first line in that loop should be to check if the object indeed has the property you've stepped into, using the Object prototype's .hasOwnProperty() method, like so:

```
function Instance(name, url, production) {
    this.name = name;
    this.url = url;
    this.production = production;
}
```

```
var myInstances = {
     'dev': new Instance('dev', 'http://sndev.service-
now.com/', false),
     'test': new Instance('test', 'http://sntest.service-
now.com/', false),
     'prod': new Instance('prod', 'http://sn.service-
now.com/', true)
};
var snInstance;
for (snInstance in myInstances) {
     if (myInstances.hasOwnProperty(snInstance) &&
myInstances[snInstance].production === true) {
          console.log('The production instance URL is: ' +
myInstances[snInstance].url);
     }
}
```

Note that the `myInstances` object consists of several other objects, generated from the `Instance` constructor/prototype. More information on constructors can be found in the **Constructors** section of this guide.

DATABASE VIEWS

It's a good idea to precede all database view names with "dv", and let the rest of the name be an indication of what tables are joined. As an example, joining the **Incident** table with the **Problem** table (for whatever reason you might do that) would result in a database view called something like **dv_incident_problem**.

As an example, joining the Incident table with the problem table (for whatever reason you might do that) would result in a database view which you might call something like **dv_incident_problem**.

DUPLICATE VARIABLES

There are *rare* circumstances where it is appropriate to have a variable (either a JS variable or a catalog variable) with a number in it. However, it is almost always best to avoid having multiple fields of the same type, with the same name, and the same purpose, such as **u_name_1** and **u_name_2**. It is understood that this is occasionally unavoidable, but if a better solution can possibly be found, that is preferable. This applies to both **names** and **labels**.

The same goes for database fields as well, and also applies to both label and name.

TABLES & COLUMNS

How not to ruin everything forever

A perfect database column is a rare thing. You could spend your whole life looking for one, and it would not be a wasted life.
—Ken Watanabe, almost

There are a lot of rules around tables and columns in ServiceNow, as in any relational database. These rules are important, since it can be very difficult (if not impossible) to change certain things about a table or field once it's created. Most of the rules will become more obvious, the more you understand about databases in general and ServiceNow in particular; however, this chapter has some general guidelines and specific advice to consider.

For table naming conventions, see the **Naming Conventions > Tables** section.

CUSTOM FIELDS

Creating custom fields is often necessary, but doing so can have serious performance implications if you're not careful, especially (*though not solely*) if it's done on the **Task** table or some other heavily extended base table. As such, you should ask yourself a few questions before adding any new database columns (AKA fields):

Is this field necessary?

Ask yourself: Does the data you expect for this field to contain actually add value in some way? What does it add? Is there a better way to add that same value, or data?

Does this data already exist somewhere else?

As we'll discuss in the **Knowing When Not to Code** section of this document, it's important to have a sense of where your data is coming from, and where else it might exist. If it already exists elsewhere, it might make sense to grab the data from there using a **reference** or **calculated** field, or even a **derived** field. If it already exists on a referenced record, it almost always makes sense to use a derived field rather than a new, custom field.

If the field should always contain a scripted or calculated value, consider using the **Calculated** check-box on the field's dictionary record, scripting the calculated value there, and setting the field to read-only on the client. Also be aware that, just like using a Business Rule, calculated field scripts only run server-side.

*For more information on calculated and default field values, see the **Tables & Columns** > **Default vs. calculated field values** section.*

Should this field appear on the form, or list?

Once you create a new field, you need to decide if it'll be shown on the form or list. Make sure you're conscious of whether or not it's on the **default** form/list view, or any **specific** views other than Default.

What label and name should I give this field?

See the ***Field names and labels*** sub-section of **the Naming Conventions** chapter of this guide for info on this.

Who should be able to see or write to this field?

If the field should not be written to, it should be made **read-only**. If it must be written to, it should be made mandatory.

If it is more than trivially important that a field be made **mandatory** or **read-only**, a server-side component such as an **ACL**, **Data Policy**, or possibly a business rule with `current.setAbortAction(true)` in conjunction with a **UI Policy** should be used in order to enforce that logic server-side as well as client-side. If it is important that some users not see the field or its value at all, then an ACL should be used. This is because any client-side measures taken to secure a field from being viewed or edited can be overridden by a sufficiently mischievous user!

Pro-tip: *If you decide to abort an operation by using* `setAbortAction()`, *you should consider adding a condition check that the source of the action is an actual logged-in user session and not an API call or automated business logic, by using* `gs.getSession().isInteractive()`. *This is great for when you want to block a user from performing an operation, but you probably don't want to interfere with back-end processes that may need to save the record.*

EXTENDING TABLES

It's important to be careful and mindful about extending tables. If you only need one or two fields from a given table, you probably don't need to extend it. If there are only a few fields you *don't* need on the other hand, you probably *should* extend it!

Keep this in mind: if table **B** extends table **A**, you will see all of the records from table **B** *as well as* all the records from table **A**, when you view table **A**. This is because tables which extend other tables, sort of exist "inside" those tables, with the extension just containing a sort of *delta*, or a list of the differences between the extended table, and the extending table.

For an example of this, navigate directly to the Task [task] table and you'll see Incidents, Change records, and Problem records among others. This is because each of those tables extends the base **Task** [task] table!

THE TASK TABLE

The **Task** [task] table in ServiceNow's "**Now**" platform is an important base table which is extended by many others. It must be handled carefully, and protected. It is important to understand that on the back-end database, the **Task** table is actually one giant, flat table. (This can change in some configurations, but this is the typical database architecture.) Because of that fact, it is important to protect the table, avoid adding unnecessary fields to it, avoid making changes on the base table itself, and generally be careful and make sure we know what we're doing when we interact with it directly.

Avoid adding long string fields to the **Task** [task] table, or tables which extend Task. Avoid creating new fields directly on the Task table, unless you're certain that you want it to be added to **every single table** which extends task. This holds true for modifying things like **labels** and **choice values** as well – unless you mean to have your change applied to all task tables (**Incident**, **Problem**, **Change**, etc.), don't make your changes on the base Task table. This is what **overrides** are for! Label overrides and dictionary overrides allow you to modify a field on just one task-based table, as opposed to on all. The same applies to any other table which extends another.

THE STATE FIELD

The **Task** table contains a field called **State** [state], which is so important that it warrants its own section. State is an **Integer** field, meaning that despite the string of text shown in the drop-down box (the field's **display value**), the actual field – both on the client, and on the server – contains an integer.

State	In Progress ▾
	New
	In Progress
	On Hold
	Resolved
	Closed
	Canceled

For this reason, and since it tends to drive the progress of a given ticket, we cannot go hacking away at the values and labels of this field. On Task-based tables in particular, there is a great deal of business logic that depends on the values in this field.

When creating new State field values, make sure that the values are numerically similar to other, similar values. For example, the OOB "**closed**" and "**cancelled**" states both have values equal to or greater than **7**. If I were to add a new state in which an Incident were no longer open, such as "**Abandoned**", I might give it a value of **9** or **10** (as "**cancelled**" has a value of **8**).

The ServiceNow "Now" platform has some built-in logic that makes a few assumptions which are important to know about when dealing with the State field:

- Any option **value** that is equal to or greater than **7** is assumed to be **inactive**.
- Any option value that is **less than** 7, is assumed to be an **active** state.

If you want to add a new "inactive" State value (meaning that the ticket should be deactivated when it's in that state) such as **Abandoned**, you should set that state's **value** to a number equal to or greater than **7** (as long as it doesn't collide with any other State value).

By the same token, if you want to add a new **active** State value (one in which the ticket's **Active** field should remain **true**), you should use a value **less than** 7. Does this mean that you can only have 6 possible **Active** State field values? Not at all! If you run out of positive numbers that are less than 7, you can simply use **negative** numbers (-**1**, -**2**, etc.).

Nowadays, there isn't a lot of logic that's hard-coded to a particular State value; however, it's still a good idea to stick with the logic that if the value is **>=7**, it's an **inactive** state, and if it's **<7**, it's an **active** state due to legacy state-handling code. The "new" method that the platform uses to determine if a state should be "closed" (deactivated) or not, is based on the State field's **close_states** dictionary attribute, which the OOB Script Include **TaskStateUtil** uses. This dictionary attribute contains a **semicolon-delimited** list of the "closed" Task states.

Attributes

default_work_state=-5,close_states=3;4;7,default_close_state=3

Also notice the **default_close_state** dictionary attribute in the above screenshot, which is also used by the **TaskStateUtil** script.

Be careful not to confuse the **Value** of a given choice option, with the **Sequence** field. The Sequence field determines the order in which the options show up in the drop-down list.

When creating a new state model for a new table, consider also creating a helper **Script Include** to keep track of the state model for you. Consider the following example:

```
var MyTaskStates = Class.create();
MyTaskStates.prototype = {
    initialize: function() {
        this.DRAFT = -1;
        this.NEW = 1;
        this.WORK_IN_PROGRESS = 2;
        this.ON_HOLD = 3;
        this.PENDING = 4;
        this.COMPLETE = 7;
        this.CANCELLED = 8;
    },

    type: 'MyTaskStates'
};
```

This is similar to the OOB Script Includes **IncidentState** and **IncidentStateSNC** (though implemented differently/more simply). You can access this state model like so:

```
var currentState = parseInt(current.getValue('state'));
if (currentState === new MyTaskStates().ON_HOLD ||
currentState === new MyTaskStates().PENDING) {
    //do something when task is on hold
}
```

It would be simple enough to create a **GlideAjax** (client-callable) version of this script as well, and that version could simply access the values in this version so you only have to maintain one script. Or you could use a Display business rule that runs on every record in your custom Task-based table, and pass the state model to the client using g_scratchpad.

DATABASE VIEWS

There are some best-practice guidelines for creating database views that we haven't yet discussed. If you are building a reporting application or working on an application which produces a dataset that may be used for reporting, you may consider using a **Database View** to present multiple tables' data coalesced together. For example, if you have an **Orders** table with a String field **User ID** that contains the User ID of the user for whom the order is placed, you may want to create a database view to "join" the Users table, and the Orders table together, so that you can report on any field on either table as though the data from both were all in one place. However, there is very often a better way.

In the example above, we should first of all be using a **Reference** field that points to the **Users** table, not a String field that contains a user's **User ID**. Once we've done that, we can simply **dot-walk** into the Users table, to grab the fields we want without using a Database View. For example, we can add a column to our report on the orders table that points to `ordered_for.department` to find the department of the user who ordered the thing, even though the department field is on the Users table, and we're reporting on the Orders table.

There are, however, some circumstances under which you must use a database view (or where it makes the most sense to use one). In these situations, there are still some additional guidelines:

- The "first" or **left** table should always be the table which we would expect to be smaller (to contain fewer records), as this makes it less database-intensive to generate the Database View.
- **Coalescing** should only be done on fields which have **database indexes**. You can find this in the table definition's related lists.
- Ensure that your table names and short-hands do not use any **SQL reserved words**. A list of reserved words can be found here: https://dev.mysql.com/doc/refman/5.7/en/keywords.html
- Non-admins do not have access to new Database Views by default, even if they would've had access to all constituent tables. Specific **ACLs** will need to be created for database views.
- Database Views can be particularly computationally intensive and are often not the best solution to a given problem. As such, it's a good idea to check with your team and/or your project's architect(s) before implementing any solutions involving a Database View prior to beginning development on it.

DEFAULT VS. CALCULATED FIELDS

It is an easy mistake to make, to think that giving a table column (AKA "**field**") a **default** value, and giving it a **calculated** value, have effectively the same result. However, this is not the case. Default and calculated values behave quite differently, and should be used for quite different purposes. In this section, we'll explore what each is (and is not) used for, and the difference in behavior between them.

DEFAULT VALUES

Default field values can be quite simple: a string, an integer, or whatever data-type matches the field's type.

Default value	This is the default value!

You can get a fair bit more advanced with it though, by using the `javascript:` keyword in the beginning of your value. Any code after the `javascript:` is executed on the server when the form loads, or when a record is inserted into the database (but not when **updated**) without a value in that field.

Default value scripts will have access to the server-side `current` object, but remember that on a **new record** form, the default value is calculated on the server, before/while the form is loaded. At that time, there is no data in the `current` object.

If there is no value in the field when it is inserted into the database, then the default value will be applied. However, if **any** data exists in the field when the record is created, the default value is not calculated or used.

Since, in addition to on insert (as long as the field is blank on insert), the default value is also calculated in order to be displayed in the "new record" form, consider the following code:

```
javascript:'Record created by ' +
gs.getUser().getDisplayName() + ' on ' +
current.getValue('sys_created_on') + '.';
```

By using the `current` object in the above code, when the form loads, we're getting a **blank** value, but the rest of our code still executes. Thus, on the new record form, we'll see a default value like this:

```
Record created by John Smith on .
```

Note the lack of the expected creation date in the string. If we were to **erase** this value on the new record form or leave it blank by creating the record in a way that doesn't use the form (such as via a script or through **list editing**), then the default value would be re-evaluated on insert, at which point there would be a `current` object for it to reference, so we **would** get the expected output in that case. However, if we load the form, get the value with the missing creation date, and then save it, then the incorrect value will be saved to the database. The default value would not be re-evaluated on insert, because the field now has a value in it!

When creating a new record from the form, the default value will be pre-populated in the field to which it applied (as we learned above). However, you can prevent this from happening so that the default value only puts data into the field on **insert** (and not on the new record form) by checking if the `current` object is populated. Here is an example using the same code as above, but wrapped in a **conditional** block that should cause it to only populate the default value if the record is being inserted into the database (when the `current` object is available):

```
javascript:if (!current.sys_created_on.nil()) { 'This record
was created by ' + gs.getUser().getDisplayName() + ' on ' +
current.getValue('sys_created_on'); }
```

This behavior is what fundamentally separates the Default value functionality from the Calculated field functionality.

CALCULATED FIELDS

While **default** values apply only on form load or on insert, and are not re-evaluated if the field is updated later or if the value changes, **calculated** fields always apply, and are re-evaluated whenever the record is updated. Also, while a field's default value may be scripted using the `javascript:` keyword, calculated fields are **always** scripted.

To enable setting a field as calculated, begin by loading the **Advanced** view of the field dictionary record, go to the **Calculated Value** form section, and check the **Calculated** box. This will enable the field calculation script editor:

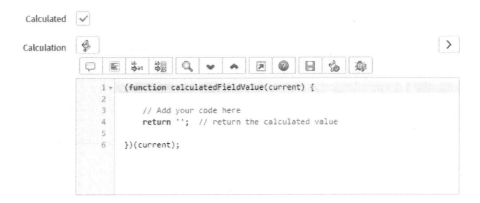

Calculated field values do have access to the `current` object (just like default value scripts), but since they are re-evaluated whenever the record is updated, it's less of an issue that the `current` object is empty when loading the **new record** form. Still though, to avoid a user seeing "*null*" in a calculated field on the new record form, it's often a good idea to put in some filler text to be displayed if the `current` object is empty, or even return a blank string in that case as you can see in the following script:

```
(function calculatedFieldValue(current) {

    var userName, updatedDate;
    if (current.sys_created_on.nil()) {
        return '';
    }
    var grUser = new GlideRecord('sys_user');
    if (grUser.get(gs.getUserID())) {
        userName = grUser.getDisplayValue();
        updatedDate = current.getValue('sys_updated_on');
        return 'Record updated by ' + userName + ' on ' +
updatedDate + '.';
    }

})(current);
```

LIST & FORM DESIGN

Guidelines for making happy users

*There are three responses to a piece of design —
yes, no, and WOW! Wow is the one to aim for.*
—Milton Glaser

Know thy users.
—Socrates, almost

U ser Interface and Form design in ServiceNow includes designs for **lists**, **forms**, **Catalog Items**, and general guidelines for building intuitive, attractive, and informative interfaces. In this chapter, we're going to learn about form and list design, layouts, and best practices.

FORM LAYOUTS

Form layouts may seem obvious, but it's often wise to take a moment to plan out how you want your forms to look, and consider some of the design guidelines that the default form views seem to adhere to. As with the rest of this document, these are **general guidelines**; not hardline rules. Form design in particular, should be more about providing a positive, functional user experience, than about sticking to black-and-white rules. If you look at a form, and it just feels *off* somehow, it probably is.

If you're creating a new table, it means you're creating a new form as well. If you're adding a field to an existing table, that might often require a form update – and it is *rarely* wise to just drop the new field at the bottom (or top) of the form. Here are some general guidelines:

Most forms that need to display enough data to warrant it, are organized into three main sections:

1. A data-dense two-column section at the top, with critical "at-a-glance" details. Fields like **Number, Assigned to,** and **Priority** usually belong at the top.
2. The middle section of a form (if the form is long enough to warrant multiple sections), is often devoted to **additional data, multi-column fields,** and other info that's good to have on the form, but not required to know at a glance.
    a. If your form has more than three sections, consider adding the additional groups as **form sections** (which may display as tabs depending on the user's preferences) in the middle grouping.
3. The last section is usually devoted to long **text** and **journal input** fields, with any **journal lists** at the very bottom of the form.
    a. You wouldn't want to have an **Activity log** in the middle of your form, because it can become quite long as activities are performed on the record; this could require a great deal of scrolling to see the rest of the fields. For this reason, the **activity** formatter should typically be one of the last elements on a form, before the related lists.
    b. Keep in mind that not all users have the **tabbed** form interface enabled, which means that if your activity section is not the last section on the form, some users will need to do a lot of scrolling,

even if it's in a separate section with other journal fields. This is usually not good.

It's rarely a good idea to put journal input fields anywhere except directly above **journal lists**; otherwise they may be mistaken for string fields, which can be very confusing.

While it doesn't have to be perfect, it's a good idea to try to design forms that are mostly **symmetrical**. This means that when using the **two-column** layout for a given section, you shouldn't put many more fields in one column than the other. Just be aware that if you have several fields in one column but only show one of them based on conditions on the form, then the form may look unbalanced in the **form designer**, but in a real-world scenario, the actual form may actually be balanced.

Ensure that you don't have the same field in two different places on the same form. Each field should only appear once on each view of the form (if at all).

If you need to modify the form for an OOB (Out-Of-Box) "admin-only" record, such as the ACL form (for example, to add a field that is not visible), be sure that it isn't captured in an **Update Set** – unless of course, you *want* it to be captured in an Update Set and propagated through the instance lifecycle! Just be mindful of whether you have an Update Set selected, and which Update Set it is. In fact, using Update Sets mindfully is probably good advice for nearly **everything** you might do in ServiceNow. It's the best way to keep your work on different projects in separate silos, and keep your instances in sync.

LIST LAYOUTS

When creating a new table, it can be easy to forget to set up the **default** list view, but this is a crucial step! If users are going to see records in your table's list, you want to provide them with as much information as is reasonable, without overcrowding the list view on a reasonably sized browser window.

Often, a unique identifying field should be shown first in the list. An example of such a field, is the **Number** field on Task-derived tables. Following that, it's usually a good idea to include other important fields that a user would likely need to see at a glance. Fields like **Assigned to** on **Task-based** tables, for example. Finally, date fields are frequently placed on the far-right, but this is by no means a requirement. The important thing is not to clutter your list view with too many fields, or include long, non-wrapped text fields that would not display enough information in the list view to be useful.

Pro-tip. In order to make a String field appear as a larger input box on the form, set its *Max length* dictionary attribute to 256 or more characters, and it will appear as a large input field automatically.

OOB RECORDS

Thinking "out of the box"

If it ain't yours, don't mess with it!
—My dad

Seriously, knock it off!
—My dad, again

Stop taking apart the neighbors' toys!!
—Still my dad

You may occasionally run into situations where you're tempted to either modify or replace an **out-of-box** record in ServiceNow, but it's important to keep a few guidelines in mind. In this chapter, we'll briefly discuss a few guidelines to consider.

For scripts in particular: **Do not modify OOB records if you can help it**! If it is an option, you may add a **condition** so the script does not run on your table, or in the circumstance you don't want it to. Then you can use **Insert and Stay** to duplicate the record, and configure it to run under the opposite condition (so it only runs when you **do** want it to).

This is important, because it's extremely difficult to know everything that might interface with, trigger, or utilize code in each script record. Modifying how it runs might very well trigger cascading bugs that will be extremely difficult to troubleshoot down the line. Also, when the instance is **upgraded** or **patched**, if one of the OOB records needs to be upgraded as part of that process, it cannot do so if the

OOB record has been modified. When we review the modifications, we'll see that only the condition has been changed, so we will keep the OOB record as-is. This protects your functionality.

Another option for **safely** replacing an OOB script's functionality, is to **deactivate** it and then create a copy of it with a different name and similar (but modified) functionality. In that case though, you would have to be very careful to watch for bugs that arise from this, if something unexpectedly tries to make use of or relies upon the old record.

Pro-tip: *It's a good idea to periodically check the system* ***warning*** *and* ***error*** *logs after each significant change to the system, and to monitor the logs in production from time to time. This will tell you if anything is misbehaving unexpectedly. By monitoring the logs closely and looking for the first instance of specific errors, you can often track down the Update Set that contained the change that caused the issue. This is also why it's a good idea to catch and log any errors you can predict in your code!*

EXTENDING OOB SCRIPT INCLUDES

For Script Includes, you can "*modify*" an OOB (or any other) Script Include, by **extending** it. Actually, extending a Script Include doesn't *actually* modify it, which is good! Instead, it involves creating a **new** Script Include that inherits the methods and properties of the one you're extending. From there, you can add new methods or properties to your Script Include, or you can override methods that were inherited from the one you're extending. It's *somewhat* rare that you should need to do this, but it's useful to understand how it is possible, so you don't have to modify an important OOB Script Include or re-implement a lot of functionality in an extant Script Include.

For an example of how this works, let's say you have the following Script Include in your instance already:

```
var ExampleScriptInclude = Class.create();
ExampleScriptInclude.prototype = {
    initialize: function() {
    },

    overrideMe: function() {
        return 'Override me!';
    },

    dontOverrideMeBro: function() {
        return this.overrideMsg;
    },

    overrideMsg: 'Don\'t override me, bro!',

    type: 'ExampleScriptInclude'
};
```

If you'd like to override or add to it, you can do so by creating a **new** Script Include, and setting the prototype to `Object.extendsObject(ExampleScriptInclude, {});`, and adding any extensions or overrides into the object in the second argument like so:

```
var ExampleExtendedScript = Class.create();
ExampleExtendedScript.prototype =
Object.extendsObject(ExampleScriptInclude, {
```

```
    overrideMe: function() {
        return 'Thanks for overriding me!';
    },

    overrideMsg: 'Thanks for not overriding me!',

    type: 'ExampleExtendedScript'
});
```

Here, we've **extended** the `ExampleScriptInclude` class in our `ExampleExtendedScript` Script Include. We've **overridden** the `overrideMe()` method (function) of that Script Include, by including a method with the **same name** in our overriding Script Include. We also override the `overrideMsg` variable, which is only used in the `dontOverrideMeBro()` method of the `ExampleScriptInclude` class!

Even though `dontOverrideMeBro()` is not in `ExampleScriptInclude`, it is still available to instances of the `ExampleScriptInclude` class because it extends (and therefore inherits the properties and methods) of `ExampleExtendedScript`. The same goes for the `overrideMsg` variable. So when we call `dontOverrideMeBro`, it uses the overridden `overrideMsg` property, and prints out the new message.

With the above two Script Includes in your instance, consider what would be output from the following code:

```
var msg = '';
var parent = new ExampleScriptInclude();
var child = new ExampleExtendedScript();

msg += '\n==Parent Script==\n' +
'Let\'s override this: \n\t' + parent.overrideMe() + '\n' +
'Don\'t override this: \n\t' + parent.dontOverrideMeBro() +
'\n';

msg += '\n==Extended/Child Script==\n' +
'Now that it\'s overridden: \n\t' + child.overrideMe() + '\n'
+
'This method wasn\'t overridden, but the property it uses
was: \n\t' + child.dontOverrideMeBro() + '\n';

gs.print(msg);
```

The results that would be printed out, look like this:

```
==Parent Script==
Let's override this:
Override me!
Don't override this:
Don't override me, bro!

==Extended/Child Script==
Now that it's overridden:
Thanks for overriding me!
This method wasn't overridden, but the property it uses was:
Thanks for not overriding me!
```

Hopefully this effectively illustrates how overrides work, and how you can extend and override OOB Script Includes, *rather* than replace or modify it. It is typically okay to extend custom (non-OOB) Script Includes in-place, but it's not usually a good idea to modify any script's methods/properties in-place, if they're already being used elsewhere.

One last thing to consider about "OOB records" is this:

Just because it's been done in the past – even if an OOB script does something a certain way, for example – it doesn't mean it's acceptable **now**. Things change, including best-practice standards, and even the underpinning architecture of the platform. For example, the change from **ES3** to **ES5** syntax support on the server, which changed how we handle lots of scripts ranging from JSON parsing and stringification, to how we interact with Arrays natively. If you don't know what the best practices are around a given technology, ask your team.

Pro-tip. *If you're still not sure, you can also ask me! Get in touch any time via Twitter at @TheTimWoodruff*

CODING GUIDELINES

Hello, World!

Always code as if the guy who ends up maintaining your code will be a violent psychopath who knows where you live.
—Martin Golding

First, solve the problem. Then, write the code.
—John Johnson

We use **JavaScript** to interact with ServiceNow, using the **Glide** API. We even use JavaScript in server-side scripts, even though ServiceNow runs Mozilla Rhino (a **Java**-based implementation of JavaScript). As with any large platform, there are certain standards and guidelines that we should do our best to follow, in order to avoid pitfalls and make sure we're building **resilient** functionality.

In this chapter, we're going to learn about some best-practices for coding with the Glide API, using JavaScript in ServiceNow specifically, and JavaScript coding in general. We'll learn how to avoid common pitfalls, and write clear, consistent, robust code that we can be proud of!

PURE FUNCTIONS

Pure functions are much easier to understand than functions that rely on state, and they tend to be much more modular as well. You don't **always** have to use pure functions, but it's usually a good idea. As with all of these guidelines, use your best judgement.

When calling a pure function with the same parameters, it always produces the same output, regardless of the state of the rest of the environment. This means the function should not have any unpredictable side-effects or rely on state data — such as time, object properties, data in the parent scope, or other variables (ones not passed in as arguments), etc.

The following function **uses**, but does not **declare** a variable called myName. It requires that a global (or parent-scope) variable called myName be declared elsewhere, and is therefore **not** a pure function:

```
function sayHello() {
    alert('Hello, ' + myName + '!');
}
```

However, if we pass in myName whenever this function is called – even if we expect this always to be the same value – we make the function much easier to read, update, and repurpose. This is what **pure** functions are all about!

```
function sayHello(myName) {
    alert('Hello, ' + myName + '!');
}
```

WRITING DRY CODE

DRY: Don't Repeat Yourself.

This is a common saying among experienced programmers, and is a good standard to code by. It means don't **rewrite** a block of code over and over, tweaking one thing in each block. There is almost always a better way.

Often, the better way involves constructing an **object** or **array** of objects with the details that change, which you use in each block, and then looping over those properties to perform the same operation with each set of data.

Consider the following code:

```
var grIncident = new GlideRecord('incident');
var encodedQuery = 'some_encoded_query_here';
grIncident.addEncodedQuery(encodedQuery);
grIncident.query();
while (grIncident.next()) {
    grIncident.setValue('state', 3); //set state to work in
progress
    grIncident.update();
}

//lather, rinse, repeat
var grProblem = new GlideRecord('problem');
var encodedQuery = 'some_encoded_query_here';
grProblem.addEncodedQuery(encodedQuery);
grProblem.query();
while (grProblem.next()) {
    grProblem.setValue('state', 4); //set state to some
other state
    grProblem.update();
}

//lather, rinse, repeat
var grChange = new GlideRecord('change_request');
var encodedQuery = 'some_encoded_query_here';
grChange.addEncodedQuery(encodedQuery);
grChange.query();
while (grChange.next()) {
    grChange.setValue('state', 5); //always specify what the
integer corresponds to when setting state
    grChange.update();
}
//[and so on...]
```

This code does the **same thing** three (or more) times, with only very minor differences in functionality each time. It is extremely inefficient to write, hard to read, and prone to errors. Imagine if you needed to make a change to the way this runs. You'd need to change it in **three** (or more) places, just to make **one** change. There's also a reasonable chance, that you or someone who comes after you, will make a mistake when making all those changes, and you'll end up with a bug that only occurs conditionally and is thus more difficult to troubleshoot.

Instead, we could construct an array of objects which contain the data that constitutes the delta between each of the code blocks above, as in the following code:

```
var i, gr, stateChangeDetails = [ //An array of objects
    {
            table_name:    'incident',
            encoded_query: 'some_query',
            state_value:    3
    },
    {
            table_name:    'problem',
            encoded_query: 'some_other_query',
            state_value:    4
    },
    {
            table_name:    'change_request',
            encoded_query: 'yet_a_third_query',
            state_value:    5
    }
];

for (i = 0; i < stateChangeDetails.length; i++) {
    gr = new GlideRecord(stateChangeDetails[i].table_name);
    gr.addEncodedQuery(stateChangeDetails[i].encoded_query);
    gr.query();
    while (gr.next()) {
            gr.setValue('state',
stateChangeDetails[i].state_value); //set state to work in
progress
            gr.update();
    }
}
```

The above code is **much** more effective, and much more **DRY**. However, there is an even better way to do this – by using constructors!

Constructors (in JavaScript) are functions which can be called with the new keyword, to return an object with the properties specified. Here's a very simple example of a constructor function:

```
function Person(name, age, coolness) {
    this.name = name;
```

```
    this.age = age;
    this.coolness = coolness;
}
```

***Note*:** *This function name (*`Person()`*) begins with a capital **P**. Unlike normal functions in JavaScript, constructors should always have names beginning with a **capital** letter.*

This function simply sets local-scope properties `name`, `age`, and `coolness`, to the values that were passed in. We don't need to return anything, since the `new` keyword sort of takes care of this for us. We can construct a new object using this constructor like so:

```
var personMe = new Person('Tim', 30, 'Extreme to the max');
```

Here, I pass in `Tim` for the name, `30` for the age, and "`Extreme to the max`" for the coolness. The resulting object looks like this, when printed out to the console:

```
Person {name: "Tim", age: 30, coolness: "Extreme to the max"}
    age: 30
    coolness: "Extreme to the max"
    name: "Tim"
```

I can figure out how any given object was constructed, by calling `.constructor.name`. In this example, that would be `personMe.constructor.name`, and would return the string "`Person`".

Of course, a constructor is a function, so you can add some fancy code into it like any other function. For example, you can specify a default value or do validation, as in the following code:

```
function Person(name, age, coolness) {
    this.name = name ? name : 'Bob'; //Default to Bob if
falsy value was passed in
    this.age = Number(age); //Cast age to a number
    this.coolness = function(coolness) { //self-executing
function to validate coolness value
        var actualCoolness = 'Total doof';
        if (coolness === actualCoolness) {
            return coolness;
        } else {
            return actualCoolness;
        }
```

```
    }(); //Adding "()" makes it execute and return the
coolness value.
}

var personMe = new Person('', '30', 'Extreme to the max');
```

You can also do other neat things with constructors, like **override** properties, **add** methods (functions contained within the objects the constructor generates), and all manner of fun stuff like that. To read more, check out the Mozilla JS docs (but remember that ServiceNow server-side code cannot run ES6 JavaScript (AKA: ECMAScript 2015). It can only process ES5 code.):

https://developer.mozilla.org/en-US/docs/Web/JavaScript/Reference/Operators/new

Now that we have an understanding of **constructors** in JavaScript, let's revisit the example earlier in this chapter. Here's the example we left off with:

```
var i, gr, stateChangeDetails = [ //An array of objects
    {
            table_name : 'incident',
            encoded_query : 'some_query',
            state_value : 3
    },
    {
            table_name:   'problem',
            encoded_query: 'some_other_query',
            state_value:   4
    },
    {
            table_name:   'change_request',
            encoded_query: 'yet_a_third_query',
            state_value:   5
    }
];

for (i = 0; i < stateChangeDetails.length; i++) {
    gr = new GlideRecord(stateChangeDetails[i].table_name);
    gr.addEncodedQuery(stateChangeDetails[i].encoded_query);
    gr.query();
    while (gr.next()) {
            gr.setValue('state',
stateChangeDetails[i].state_value); //set state to work in
progress
            gr.update();
    }
}
```

This is better than how it was originally, but it still requires re-typing a lot of stuff, like property names. If we were to re-write this using a **constructor** to build each object, it would look like this instead:

```
var i, gr, stateChangeDetails;
//constructor
function StateChangeDetail(table, query, state) {
    this.table_name = table;
    this.encoded_query = query;
    this.state_value = state;
}
stateChangeDetails = [ //An array of StateChangeDetail
objects
    new StateChangeDetail('incident', 'some_query', 3),
    new StateChangeDetail('problem', 'some_other_query', 4),
    new StateChangeDetail('change_request', 'third_query',
5)
];

for (i = 0; i < stateChangeDetails.length; i++) {
    gr = new GlideRecord(stateChangeDetails[i].table_name);
    gr.addEncodedQuery(stateChangeDetails[i].encoded_query);
    gr.query();
    while (gr.next()) {
            gr.setValue('state',
stateChangeDetails[i].state_value); //set state to work in
progress
            gr.update();
    }
}
```

In the above code, on *line 3*, we declare our constructor, which takes three arguments: `table`, `query`, and `state`. From those, it constructs an object with three properties: `table_name`, `encoded_query`, and `state_value`. Then, on *lines 8-12*, we build an array of objects generated from that constructor, using the `new` keyword.

Finally, on *lines 14-22*, we loop over the array, and access the elements of the objects to do the work we need to do.

PASS-BY-REFERENCE

One thing to note about dealing with functions, scope, and objects in general in JavaScript, is an oddity of the language called **pass-by-reference**. This is probably one of the most important guidelines in this book, yet it might also be the least adhered to.

Consider the following code:

```
var coolness = 'Extreme to the max';
changeCoolness(coolness);
console.log(coolness);

function changeCoolness(coolness) {
    var actualCoolnessLevel = 'Total doofus';
    coolness = actualCoolnessLevel;
}
```

In this code, I'm declaring my coolness to be **Extreme to the max** on *line 1*, but since I probably shouldn't rely on my mom's opinion, I pass coolness into a function called changeCoolness(), which modifies the variable we've passed into it, and sets it to my *actual* coolness level. This function does not return a value, it simply modifies it and then ends.

Since the value we passed into this function is a **primitive** (a *string, number,* or *Boolean*), passing it into the changeCoolness() function creates a new variable with a **copy** of the value from the coolness variable, in the scope of the function. Because of this, when we print out the value of coolness on *line 3*, we see that the value has not actually changed. Despite being modified in the scope of the changeCoolness() function, the value that prints out on *line 3* is still "**Extreme to the max**".

This is as you would probably expect this code to behave. However, for non-primitive variable types, this behaves almost exactly **opposite** from how you might expect!

First, let's just clarify what **non-primitive** values are: A non-primitive value is essentially anything that isn't a *string, boolean, number, null,* or *undefined*. Anything that isn't one of those five data-types, is technically an **Object**. This includes *objects* (obviously), *arrays, functions, prototypes,* and lots of other types of stuff. The following object, called me, is an example of a non-primitive value. There's nothing special about it that makes it non-primitive; **all** objects are non-primitive.

```
var me = {
    name : 'Tim',
    age : 30,
    coolness : 'Extreme to the max'
};
```

Let's take our code from the previous example, which you'll recall did **not** modify the `coolness` variable in-place, and let's try the same thing using the above non-primitive **object**. Here's the code:

```
var me = {
    name : 'Tim',
    age : 30,
    coolness : 'Extreme to the max'
};

changeCoolness(me);
console.log('I\'m this cool: ' + me.coolness);

function changeCoolness(person) {
    var actualCoolnessLevel = 'Total doofus';
    person.coolness = actualCoolnessLevel;
}
```

Consider the above code carefully. What do you think will happen when we print out the value of the coolness property on *line 8*?

You may be surprised to find that even though the only place where the value was changed was in the scope of the function (which never returned a value), the string **Total doofus** will print out! This is because when we passed the argument `me` into the `changeCoolness()` function, we actually passed a **reference** to the object. That means that the variable `person` in the function, and the variable `me` in the parent scope, both literally refer to the **same object** in memory!

I don't mean that both variables "contain an object with the same value", I mean they both contain a reference to literally the same object. Whatever you do to one variable, you do to the other, because they are *literally* the same.

Am I saying the word "literally" too much?

This has major implications for how your code functions, both for abstract objects, and for doing things like working with `GlideRecord` and `GlideElement` objects, and especially for loops. It wouldn't be incorrect to use either **pass-by-reference** (with *objects*, *functions*, etc.), or **pass-by-value** (with *primitives*), but it is important to understand the differences in **behavior**. More information on this concept, and a helpful article with more examples, can be found in the section **Getting and setting field values.**

GETTING AND SETTING FIELD VALUES

When working with **GlideRecord** objects, it's common to either get or set the value of a specific field. To do that, it's important to use a **getter** (`.getValue()`) and setter (`.setValue()`). This section explains why and how in more detail. The important takeaway is to avoid using notation like `gr.field_name` which directly accesses the **GlideElement** object for the field. Every field in a **GlideRecord** object (whether it's "`current`" in a business rule, or "`grIncident`" in a Script Include, is itself, another **object** (a type called **GlideElement**). So if I write `var shortDesc = gr.short_description;`, I'm actually setting the variable `shortDesc` to a **reference** to the **GlideElement** object located at `gr.short_description`. If that value changes, so does your variable, because JavaScript uses **pass-by-reference** (PBR). (More on PBR in the Pass-by-Reference section).

For this reason, we should virtually always use the `.getValue()` method of GlideRecords to retrieve a value, and `.setValue()` to set a value. There are three exceptions to this:

1. **Journal fields**: To interact with a journal field, just access it directly (e.g. `current.work_notes = 'note';`).
2. **Catalog variables**: To interact with catalog or record producer variables, access them directly. However, use the `.toString()` method to ensure that you get a **primitive** and avoid pass-by-reference issues. (e.g. `current.variables.requested_for.toString();`)
3. **Dot-walking**: Using `.toString()` is also a good means of getting a **primitive** value from a **dot-walked** field (E.g. `current.request.short_description.toString()`). Just remember not to dot-walk through more than three layers. If you must dot-walk more than three layers, use the `.getReference()` API of the GlideElement object instead. If doing this client-side, be sure to use a callback function (more info in the client/server section).

The really important thing about using `.getValue()` specifically, is to get a primitive value and avoid **pass-by-reference**, which can quickly weave a tangled web of references and unexpected behaviors. The `.getValue()` API is the best-practice way of doing this, but you can also use `gr.field_name.toString()`, as mentioned above.

You may occasionally be tempted to use `gr.field_name + ''` which relies on JavaScript's **implicit type-coercion** functionality, which is... fine... but there have been issues, as JavaScript's type-coercion can be unexpected, especially if you have a more complex statement. Further, since your server-side code is actually evaluated in Rhino (through a layer of Java, which does not have implicit type coercion), you may end up with a "serialized character array" rather than a String, which is complicated and bad. The best-practice and most efficient way to retrieve a primitive value, is nearly always to use `.getValue()`.

CONSISTENCY

It's important to be **consistent**, at least within any one script, even when it comes to things beyond normal coding and naming conventions. One example of this, is **string delimiters**.

Technically, JavaScript will handle any unique string declaration so long as the beginning and ending quote-marks match, and it will ignore any others. For example, consider the following script:

```
var goodToKnow = 'Even though this string contains "double-
quotes", I don\'t have to escape them, ' +
'because the string began with a single-quote. \n' +
'I do however, have to escape apostrophes, or the interpreter
will think I\'m ending my string.' +
"If I wanted to switch to double-quotes mid-string, I could
(using the plus operator), and then I " +
"wouldn't have to escape the apostrophe/single-quote
anynmore, but would have to escape double-quotes." +
"But if I did that, I'd surely annoy whoever tried to update
my code later on!";
```

Personally, I – your fearless author - use single-quotes (like 'this') as opposed to double-quotes (like "this"). This is because the double-quote takes an extra keystroke (**SHIFT**), and **I'm extraordinarily lazy**... Just kidding; it's because I declare strings more frequently than I use conjunctions within them, which would require escaping the apostrophes, as in the word `isn\'t`; so it makes sense for me. If you prefer to use **double-quotes** (""), that is also fine! Just make sure you're **consistent** within your scripts. The same goes for any other optional conventions. Whenever you have options, be sure to be consistent!

The same rules about consistency apply to things like curly-brace placement. It's a good idea to maintain consistency within your own code and, as much as possible, within the instance as a whole, as to things like curly-brace placement. For example, the following code demonstrates a **non-standard** way of writing a conditional block:

```
if (recordIsValid){
//do something with the record
}

else
{
//throw an error message
}
```

This is a little more difficult to follow, because the curly-brace placement is **inconsistent**, and there is a white-space (line break) gap between the 'if' and 'else' blocks, which makes it much harder to follow. Instead, here is the more commonly accepted standard way of writing a conditional block:

```
if (recordIsValid) {
    //do something with the record
} else {
    //throw an error message
}
```

Finally, ensure that your **indentation** is consistent. The default ServiceNow IDE is not great at indentation, so be sure to click the "Format Code" ☰ button on the IDE, and visually scan through your code for indentation/spacing/line-break issues before saving it.

FIELD SECURITY VS. FIELD OBSCURITY

It may be tempting to exclusively use UI Policies, to control field visibility and mandatory state – they're just so convenient! - but whether you're talking about **UI Policies** or **Client Scripts**, it's important to realize that any **client-side-only** measures you take to make a field *invisible*, *mandatory*, or *read-only*, can be **thwarted** by a user with a browser! In fact, on rare occasion (such as if the user has a slow internet connection, or there is an error in an early loading client script), a field that's meant to be read-only may not appear that way right away, and could be edited.

45

Pro-tip. *Hiding a field does not clear its value! If you initially show a field, then conditionally hide it, but the user had entered a value whilst it was visible, that value will still be in the field, and it'll be saved to the database and potentially trigger logic too!*

Any **client-side** measures to protect data, that aren't backed by a **server-side** component such as a *Business Rule*, *ACL*, or *Data Policy*, **can be bypassed**. Normally this is not a big deal. Some field protections are matters of convenience, or at least would not result in detrimental issues if the client-side field protections were ignored. However, in some cases (such as with approval records), field security can be highly important.

Before committing to only using client-side field protection measures such as a *UI Policy* or *Client Script*, ask yourself what the impact would be if a user were to ignore those protections. If the answer is "major impact", you should definitely consider an *ACL*, *Data Policy*, or possibly even a *Business Rule* to protect your data integrity instead.

CLIENT SCRIPTS & FIELD-LEVEL SECURITY

It's usually best not to use **Client Scripts** to control field *visibility*, *mandatory* state, or *read-only* state; however, there are exceptions. For example, highly complex logic sometimes cannot be accommodated by one UI Policy. Complex multi-field conditions sometimes also cannot be accommodated.

If you must use a Client Script instead of a UI Policy for some reason, be sure to document your reasons for doing so in your code or description, so other developers can understand why you did what you did. Also make sure that you have some logic in the client script that emulates what would be the "**reverse if false**" condition in a UI Policy (if the actions should be reversed if the condition is false), or at least provide some logic for how to behave when the condition is not (or is no longer) true.

As a general rule, best practice dictates that if a UI Policy can do the job without an inordinate amount of fuss, use that over a Client Script.

SETVISIBLE() VS. SETDISPLAY()

On the rare occasion that you need to hide a field using a Client Script, it is important to understand the difference between the setVisible() and setDisplay() methods of the g_form object in Client Scripts.

setVisible() hides the element inside the section, but leaves a blank space where the element was. I can imagine some situations where this might be desired, but most commonly you'll want the entire section where the field or variable was, to disappear. In this case, you would use setDisplay(). setVisible() and setDisplay() set the actual document element's visible and display properties respectively, which is the reason for the difference in behavior. It relates to the difference in behavior of those field attributes. See the screenshots below for examples.

Before running the script:

Requested for	Tim S. Woodruff	
Location	United States	
Due date	2018-02-01 10:50:28	

After running `g_form.setVisible(fieldName, false);`:

| Requested for | Tim S. Woodruff | |

| Due date | 2018-02-01 10:50:28 | |

Note the blank space where the field once was

After running `g_form.setDisplay(fieldname, false);`:

| Requested for | Tim S. Woodruff | |
| Due date | 2018-02-01 10:50:28 | |

Note that the field and the space it occupied are now both gone

AJAX & DISPLAY BUSINESS RULES

There are a multitude of reasons you might need to communicate between the client, and the server (such as in a *Client Script, Catalog Client Script,* or *UI Policy*), including:

- Retrieving a **system property** to determine whether a field should be visible
- Checking some value on another record in another table
- Retrieving the GlideRecord object for a record being referenced on a form
- Dealing with date/time objects, and calculating system time

With the notable exception of certain Client Scripts which must run on **submit**, it's always important to make sure we're performing **asynchronous** server requests in client-side code. In most cases, this can be done by specifying a **callback function** (such as when using the GlideRecord `.query()` method client-side), or by using **GlideAjax**.

Pro-tip: It's not within the scope of this handbook, but if you're not sure how to make your request run asynchronously, we've written a whole article on the topic over here: http://ajax.sngeek.com/

If you know **in advance** that you're going to need certain information every time a given form is loaded, you can use a **Display Business Rule** to grab the data from the server as the form loads, and pass it up to the client. Display Business Rules are a special type of script that run on the **server** when you request a record's data from the server in order to load a form.

Once your browser requests the page and record from the database to display in the form, the Display Business Rule runs on the server if the record you're loading matches the condition in the business rule. In that script, you'll have access to the object `g_scratchpad`. You can add properties to this object in the *Display Business Rule,* and these properties will be available to any *client script, UI Policy,* or *UI Action* running on that form via the same `g_scratchpad` object.

Note: This does not work for Catalog Client Scripts. You'll have to rely on asynchronous AJAX requests to the server in that case.

Display Business Rules are probably the most effective and **efficient** way of retrieving data from the server, but they are sometimes overkill. For example, if you only need the data that you would load into g_scratchpad in one special circumstance based on some rare client-side event, it might make sense to use a **GlideAjax** call instead. Just make sure that it's asynchronous!

GlideAjax is the second most efficient means of retrieving data from the server. However, unlike Display Business Rules, GlideAjax requires both a client-side, *and* a server-side component, so it can be a bit more complicated.

Pro tip: If you look up the documentation on GlideAjax, you'll find that you can add "nodes" to the returned AJAX, which is useful for returning multiple/complex values from a single call. However, a much easier and cleaner way of doing this, is to return an object populated with the values you need stored in properties. The object will then be available when you get the 'answer' node of the returned XML, and you can work with it directly. Much simpler! More details on this, GlideAjax, and asynchronicity in general, in the article at http://ajax.sngeek.com/

Finally, the least efficient method that's still acceptable in a pinch, is an **asynchronous** GlideRecord call. The same article linked above, will walk you through how to make a GlideRecord call happen asynchronously. You can also find documentation on all of these APIs in the ServiceNow developer site, for specifics on how to use them.

To reiterate: If you know exactly what data you need to retrieve from the server in advance, and the conditions under which you want to retrieve the data are known on load, a **Display Business Rule** is probably the best option. If not, **GlideAjax** is likely the best option. For small, efficient queries (such as only returning one record), an asynchronous **GlideRecord** query can be used. For getting a GlideRecord object from a **reference** field, calling `g_form.getReference()` with a **callback function** makes the query asynchronous, and is also acceptable (especially if you're only retrieving a single record).

DOM MANIPULATION

In the **Service Portal** (The "Now" platform's fancy new user-friendly front-end), DOM (Document Object Model) manipulation is almost entirely deprecated. There are ways around it, but ServiceNow officially recommends avoiding it at virtually all costs; not just in the Service Portal but, for future compatibility reasons, everywhere.

For this reason, it's important to use OOB methods whenever possible, that allow you to avoid DOM manipulation. The same applies to synchronous GlideRecord queries, and GlideAjax calls. Even in onSubmit Catalog Client Scripts. This means that we need to develop work-arounds for certain bits of functionality which required either synchronicity, or DOM access. A great example of this, is requiring attachments on submission of a catalog item.

*Note: The best method that I've been able to come up with for validating attachments in the Service Portal, has a Script Include component, and a **JS Include**. This enables a specific API in the Service Portal:* `sp_form.getAttachments()`. *This API is not available out-of-box and must be implemented to work. You can find details on how to implement it at http://portalattachments.sngeek.com/.*

For a Catalog Client Script to work in the Service Portal, it needs to be set to a type of either "All" or "Mobile/Service Portal". If the latter is selected, it will **only** work in the Service Portal. Virtually all Catalog Client Scripts should have their **type** field set to **All**, but one exception is if you have one script to provide certain functionality in the "desktop"/classic view, and another corresponding script to enable that functionality in the Service Portal. If this is the case, be sure to document that in your code so other developers will know what's going on if they read it!

WHEN *NOT* TO CODE

Making your code effective and efficient is important, but it's also important to ask yourself a few questions **before** writing a custom script to solve a problem.

As we've discussed elsewhere in this guide, many of the custom scripted solutions that could be done via Client Scripts, can also (and should) be done via UI Policies; and while there are some situations where using a Client Script instead is just fine, UI Policies are usually the way to go.

The same logic applies to Business Rules: While a custom scripted solution (AKA: An **Advanced** Business Rule) is sometimes necessary, it's surprisingly often that you'll find you can actually use the **Actions** tab the Business Rule form, and perform simple operations there.

For example, say you have a catalog task, and you want it to be assigned to the same user as the parent RITM. You could write a script to do that, or much more preferably, you could use Actions on a Business Rule like so:

On a related note: If you find yourself setting a field (especially a custom field) to the same value as another field in a dot-walked record, you should carefully consider whether the field itself is actually **necessary**. Very often, it can be replaced with a **derived** field. For example, consider the **Catalog Task** [sc_task] table again. Imagine we wanted to display the **Short Description** of the RITM, on the sc_task form. Well, we could create a new custom field called "RITM Short Description" [u_ritm_short_description], and populate it using a client-side GlideAjax call, or a Business Rule's **Actions** tab, but if we did that, an architect might later come by and hit us with a *101-key PS/2 IBM Model M buckling-spring keyboard*. Since those are very heavy, it would make far more sense to simply open the **Form Layout** tool, and add a derived field (AKA: a dot-walked field) that points to `request_item.short_description`.

Note: Unfortunately, there has been a "bug" in ServiceNow for some time, that you cannot set a field on a record in another table by using dot-walking in the Actions tab of a business rule. You can get a value from a related record by dot-walking, but not set one. For that, you'll have to use a script.

DEBUGGING

When troubleshooting the behavior of a script or object, remember to check the basics first. If you aren't sure what's causing some behavior, start by **disabling** the object you think is causing it, and see if that resolves it. If not, that object *probably* isn't the culprit. Additionally, don't forget to consider the **other** scripts that could be triggered if your script changes something in a form or field! Business Rules might be running whenever you make a change, and that could be the true root of a given problem.

Using the "debugging" tools built into ServiceNow is a great way to find out what's going on when you're not sure what script might be causing some behavior you're seeing. The debugging tools can be found in the Application Navigator, under **System Diagnostics > Session Debug**.

TESTING

The art of not looking like a dolt

Pay attention to zeros. If there is a zero, someone will divide by it.
—Cem Kaner

Before software can be reusable, it has first to be usable.
—Ralph Johnson

TESTING is arguably one of the most important parts of the software development process, but it can also be one of the most tedious. It is important though, as you might be surprised how often even veteran developers find defects in their development. Finding bugs doesn't make you a bad developer – it makes you a good one!

In this chapter, we'll learn about *how* to test our code, as well as how to both prevent errors, and catch them when they happen anyway.

TESTING EXECUTION PATHS

It's important to **always test your execution paths**. An execution path is a logical "route" that a given bit of code could take, based on the **control flow** in the code. Control flow consists of any code which is evaluated to determine the path of execution your code goes down. if/else blocks are probably the most ubiquitous examples of control flow.

If you're writing a script, it almost goes without saying that you should give it a quick test to make sure it's working before moving on. However, what if your code has multiple **execution paths**? That is, what if your code does one thing in one set of circumstances, and another thing in another set of circumstances?

In that case, it's important (and wise) to test each path of execution that your code could take (each condition in the flow-control of your code).

Consider the following code:

```
if (g_form.getValue('state') === 3) {
    /* Do a thing */
} else if (g_form.getValue('state') === 4) {
    /* Do something different */
} else {
    /* Do yet a third thing */
}
```

After saving the above Client Script, I might test it by first setting the value of the **state** field to 3, and making sure the appropriate code ran without errors, then setting it to 4 and checking, then setting it to something that's neither, and validating that the code in the else block also fires correctly. I would watch my testing browser's **console** for any errors that seemed related to my code, or – if I were writing server-side code – I would watch the **system logs**. Doing **anything less than this**, risks non-functional code getting into production, and making you look very silly indeed.

*Note: Don't forget to test an execution path that your code should **not** execute under as well! You don't want to verify that your code works in all the circumstances you expect it to, only to find after releasing it into production, that it also executes when you **don't** want it to!*

IMPERSONATION

It may be tempting to take the perspective "I'm a developer, not a QA tester!", but if your work comes back from testing, it takes more time overall and more effort on your part. Plus, it doesn't look great having your work fail testing.

Simply taking the extra step of impersonating a user who you know should have the relevant permissions will go a long way to ensuring that your work doesn't fail testing, but it's also a good idea – if applicable – to test as a user that should **not** be able to see or do whatever it is you've built.

To that end, it's not a bad idea to see if your organization would be willing to add an optional **Testing user** field to the table in which you track your development stories.

Pro-tip: Open an "Incognito" or "Private" browser tab and log into your ServiceNow instance there. In that tab, you can impersonate the testing user without impacting your other browser session.

ERRORS

An important part of the testing process, is looking for errors. Not errors in functionality (though those are obviously also important to identify), but errors in your code. Even if your code *seems* to behave correctly, you may still have some code that throws errors.

While running your tests, it's a good idea to open your browser's **console** window and watch for any errors or warnings that show up. Any time your code performs any server-side operations, it's also a good idea to check the system error logs from **System Logs > System Log > Errors.**

To prevent hard errors in your code, and to handle *anticipated unexpected* situations, consider using a `try{}catch(){}` block. For example, if you expect a specific method to be present on some object, you may be pretty confident that it's there, but you can **anticipate** the *unexpected* scenario in which it's undefined by putting your code in a `try{}` block, and using the `catch(){}` block to "handle" the error by throwing a specific message to the console (using `console.error()`) or system error logs (using `gs.error()`). The up-side of handling errors in this way, is that when you've **caught** an error, you can determine what to do after that. For example, consider the following code:

```
try {
    var priorityElement = gel("incident.priority");
    setPriorityBackgroundColor(priorityElement);
} catch(ex) {
    console.warn('Unable to get priority element or set
element color. Using alternative handling');
    alternateIndicatePriority(); //optional
}
```

The above code attempts to use the `gel()` API to get the Incident priority field element. However, this API is not always available (for example, on the Service Portal). If this API is undefined, this would throw an error. By capturing that error in a `try{}` block, we can determine how to handle the error ourselves. The code in the `catch(){}` block will only fire in the event that the code in the `try{}` block throws an error. This allows us to use some alternative functionality for when `gel()` isn't available.

If you know that your code may run where a certain API is unavailable, or if you know that your code otherwise might run into an error, it is preferable to **prevent** the error rather than **catch** it. For example, if this were a Catalog Client Script which we expected to at least occasionally be run in the Service Portal (where the `gel()` API is not available), we might rewrite this code as follows:

```
if (typeof gel !== 'undefined') {
    try {
        var priorityElement = gel("incident.priority");
        setPriorityBackgroundColor(priorityElement);
    } catch(ex) {
        console.warn('Unable to get priority element or
set element color. Using alternative handling');
        alternateIndicatePriority('some error message');
//optional
    }
} else {
    alternateIndicatePriority('some other error message');
}
```

Above, we're still using the try/catch (because developing **defensive** code is usually a good idea), but we're doing so inside a condition which should **prevent** the `catch{}` block from being triggered most of the time.

System Diagnostics

▼ Session Debug

Enable All

Disable All

Debug Business Rule

Debug Business Rule (Details)

Debug Log

Debug SQL

Debug SQL (Detailed)

Debug Security

Debug Escalations

Debug Text Search

Debug UI Policies

Disable UI Policies Debug

Debug Data Policies

Debug Quotas

Debug Homepage Render

Debug Scopes

Debug Date/Time

Debug Metric Statistics

CODE DOCUMENTATION

Not just *what*, but *how*

Ink is better than the best memory.
—Chinese proverb

I have no idea what's going on here.
—Developers everywhere

Documenting your code is arguably one of the most important things that you can do—Period. Even if your code doesn't work, **well-documented** code will allow another developer to at least understand what you were going for.

Nearly every time you write code, you should be **documenting** that code. This takes the form of leaving actual comments in and around your code, as well as being sure to write "self-documenting" code (more on that shortly). It is important to do both!

"Code documentation" refers to explanatory text within your code. This generally takes three main forms, which we'll learn about in this chapter: Your variable names, structure, and syntax, comments within your code, and specialized comments called **JSDoc**.

SELF-DOCUMENTING CODE

Self-documenting code is, at its core, a best-practice way of naming things so that it's clear what they contain and what they're going to be used for. This is the bare minimum that you should be doing in order to make your code clear, readable, and extensible.

Writing self-documenting code doesn't mean that you don't have to write any actual comments in your code! In fact, **most** code you write should have something explaining what it is and how it works, even if it's highly obvious, just so the next person to read it doesn't go down a rabbit hole, seeking non-existent complexity. Code comments and self-documenting code are two methods of documentation that work **together** to make your code easily readable and updatable.

Self-documenting code can be broken down into three main components:
- Structure
- Naming
- Syntax

STRUCTURE

Self-documenting code begins with a clear structural outline that makes sense and flows **logically**. This means breaking out major stand-alone and often-utilized functionality into **functions** that can be called using intelligently-chosen, clear, concise names. This applies especially for functionality which, when simply written out, isn't very clear. Take the following line of code for example:

```
var w = m/60/24/7*0.001;
```

At a glance, it's not totally clear what's going on here. To make it clearer, we could re-write it like this:

```
var milSeconds = 3200000;
var weeks = getWeeksFromMS(milSeconds);
function getWeeksFromMS(milSeconds) {
    var seconds = milSeconds * 0.001;
```

```
    var minutes = seconds / 60;
    var hours = minutes / 60;
    var days = hours / 24;
    var weeks = days / 7;
    return weeks;
}
```

This is a LOT more clear, if not the most efficient way of writing this function (at least in terms of keystrokes). Instead, let's add some code comments to make things a lot more clear without needing to perform so many separate operations, and initialize so many variables:

```
var milSeconds = 3200000; //3.2 million milliseconds
var weeks = getWeeksFromMS(milSeconds);

function getWeeksFromMS(milSeconds) {
    //Multiply by 0.001 to get seconds, divide by 60 to get
minutes, 60 again to
    // get hours, then by 24 to get days, and by 7 to get
weeks, which we return.
    return milSeconds * 0.001 / 60 / 60 / 24 / 7;
}
```

In the above code, we use multiple code documentation methods to make our code both clear, and succinct. Not only have we added actual **comments** to our code to explain what it's doing, but we've broken out the functionality of converting milliseconds into weeks, into a separate **function** with a **name** that makes it clear what it does. This way, unless it isn't working, we can look at just the first **two lines** of our code and have a good idea of what's going on here.

We've seen how, by making our code more **functional** (moving functionality into intelligently named functions), we can make our code clearer. But there is another opportunity for *functionalizing* and clarifying our code, which involves functionalizing certain **conditional expressions**. Consider the following code for an example of how we might improve:

```
if (!g_form.getValue('needs_repair') &&
!g_form.getValue('needs_replacement')) {
    g_form.showFieldMsg('additional_info', 'Please clarify
what action is required', 'info', false);
}
```

In the code above, the condition in the `if` block is not too terribly complex, but its use of the `&&` operator along with the `!` negator may be confusing. Instead, it might be clearer if we wrote it like so:

```
if (!needsRepairOrReplacement()) {
    g_form.showFieldMsg('additional_info', 'Please clarify
what action is required', 'info', false);
}

function needsRepairOrReplacement() {
    return (g_form.getValue('needs_repair') !== '' ||
g_form.getValue('needs_replacement') !== '');
}
```

Even though it's technically more lines of code, it's much clearer what's going on. We've **abstracted** the bother of checking each field individually into a function, so as long as that function acts as expected, we can treat it like a black box that always returns what we're looking for. Of course, you can't always communicate everything about how your function works just by the naming convention; and that's where JSDoc comes in (see the section on JSDoc a little later in this chapter).

In this case though, we can make things even more simple by replacing the function itself, with a **variable**, like so:

```
var needsRepairOrReplacement =
(g_form.getValue('needs_repair') !== '' ||
g_form.getValue('needs_replacement') !== '');

if (!needsRepairOrReplacement) {
    g_form.showFieldMsg('additional_info', 'Please clarify
what action is required', 'info', false);
}
```

One last piece of advice when it comes to self-documenting code structure, is to **group** your statements logically. One example of that, which you may be familiar with, is initialization of variables. In JavaScript, the **interpreter** always groups variable initialization at the top of the scope, so if we want our code to be written in a way that matches the way it'll execute, we group initialization at the beginning like so:

```
function howAreYa(myName) {
    var response;
    var greeting = 'Hello, ' + myName;
    var question = 'How are ya?';

    alert(greeting);
    response = prompt(question);
    alert('You said: ' + response);
}
```

That extra line-break in the middle visually separates the variable initialization and declaration block from the actual functionality of alerting and prompting the user. That makes it much easier to read, update, and troubleshoot! It also more closely reflects how the code will *actually execute* in the user's browser and it's helpful to prevent initialization of variables inside loops and attempting to use uninitialized variables that would only have been initialized inside conditional blocks.

NAMING

In addition to what we discussed in the **Naming Conventions** section of this compendium, the way you name primitive variables, functions, and other objects can also contribute to how "self-documenting" your code is. Avoid using vague terms like "handle" or "manage". For example, `handleGlideRecords()` is a lot **less clear** than `convertGlideRecordToObject()` (for which, by the way, there is an OOB API for in the `GlideRecordUtil` Class: `.toHashMap()`).

For your functions, make sure they do one specific thing, and name them using active verbs like `sendFile()` or `convertXML()`. Make sure to contain **just** that functionality inside that function. If you need to add more functionality, that's fine, but you should accomplish that by returning something from the first function, and then potentially passing that something into the next step function. There are exceptions to this rule (as with all rules), but it'll help you out a lot to be mindful of this standard.

An example of what to try to avoid would be something like this:

```
validateRecord(record);

function validateRecord(record) {
    var recordIsValid = record.isValid() && record.active;
    if (recordIsValid) {
        updateRecord(record);
    }
}
function updateRecord(record) {
    if (record.update('something')) {
        return true;
    }
}
```

Pro-tip. In JavaScript, as long as there's only one line that executes following a conditional statement (`if()`), you technically don't have to include the curly braces. However, we **strongly recommend** that you do anyway; first, because it's **much** easier to read this way, and second because it's much easier and less confusing to update the functionality by adding additional statements in the conditional code block when the curly braces already exist.

In this example, our executing code calls a function: `validateRecord()`. This function then calls another function to **update** the record: `updateRecord()`; but in our main top-level code, we haven't called the `updateRecord()` function, so a developer would have to **search through this code** to find out when and how the record is being updated, if they noticed it at all! This code's behavior doesn't make sense at first glance because the `validateRecord()` function is not only validating the record, but updating it too – which is contraindicated by its name.

Instead, we should do something closer to this:

```
if (validateRecord(record)) {
    updateRecord(record);
}

function validateRecord(record) {
    return record.isValid() && record.getValue('active') ===
'true';
}

function updateRecord(record) {
    if (record.update('reason for update')) {
        return true;
    }
    return false;
}
```

As you can see, it's much easier to understand what's going on here without having to investigate each function individually for additional **undocumented** (or at least, not self-documenting) functionality. Imagine if you look into function **a**, and learn that it uses function **b**, and function **b** uses function **c**, and so on. Tracing down the source of a bug in code like that would be a **nightmare**!

Note: In the above code, as with most code samples in this document, we're not including *JSDoc* documentation, and may not be following one or two other best-practices. That's because I want to keep my sample code *succinct,* easy to read quickly, and to highlight the specific point that the sample is meant to demonstrate. Please do not model your code *precisely off any one snippet of sample code here. Instead, focus on the specific lesson it's trying to demonstrate.*

Another good practice when it comes to naming variables, is to indicate the units of the variable. For example, instead of `time`, consider using `timeInSeconds`; `widthPx` instead of `width`.

SYNTAX

When it comes to syntax, different coding languages have different syntactical tricks you can use. A few of these are mostly common knowledge and can make your code more clear. For example, **ternary** statements can be very useful if used only in the correct circumstances (and not chained, which can make them quite confusing).

By the same token though, some syntactical tricks are more **arcane**, less well-known, and less supported. It's a good idea to avoid tricks like this. For example:

```
isValidRecord && updateRecord();
```

Instead, it's **usually** best to stick with the more clear, compatible, and common:

```
if (isValidRecord) {
    updateRecord();
}
```

CODE COMMENTS

In addition to writing self-documenting code, it is important to leave **comments** in your code, indicating what's going on; especially when it otherwise might not be totally clear. Most scripts you write should contain **some** comments.

If you leave a code comment that is long enough to wrap to the next line, consider placing it in a "block-comment" above the code to which it applies, and using a manual line-break to wrap it, as in the following:

```
/*
This is a block comment about what the below
function does, and what it returns into the
hasThingBeenDone variable.
```

63

```
*/
var hasThingBeenDone = doAThing();
```

You might also do a manual line-break before the line of code auto-wraps, and putting the next line in a separate comment using //. This is usually more readable, which is what code comments are all about!

Consider ways to make effective use of comments (and **well-named** variables) to make your code clearer. Consider the following line of code:

```
gr.addEncodedQuery('active=true^assignment_group=fe7204496fd1
5e00b7e659212e3ee4e1^additional_assignee_listLIKE536968cd6f9b
21008ca61e250d3ee4d1');
```

This doesn't make it very clear what we're doing, because as a developer looking at this code in 2 years, I'm not going to know what the sys_id values correspond to; but what if we wrote it out like this instead:

```
//Group: ServiceNow Dev Team
var assignmentGroup = 'fe7204496fd15e00b7e659212e3ee4e1';
//Assignee: John D Smith
var assignee = '536968cd6f9b21008ca61e250d3ee4d1';
var incidentQuery = 'active=true^assignment_group=' +
assignmentGroup + '^additional_assignee_listLIKE' + assignee;

gr.addEncodedQuery(incidentQuery);
```

This way is more verbose, but much more clear, and it gives us an opportunity to document what each sys_id corresponds to.

*Note: Hard-coding Sys IDs is often not a good idea. Sometimes it's unavoidable, but if you can extrapolate or programmatically determine the record you want the sys_id for, this is usually better. Consider having an **assignee's** Sys ID hard-coded in scripts throughout a workflow, and then the person to whom that Sys ID corresponds, leaves the company! Something like a **System Property** would usually be a better choice in cases like this, so you can modify it in just one place!*

JSDOC

JSDoc is a **standards-based markup language** used to annotate JavaScript source code. Using comments containing JSDoc, you can add documentation describing the interface(s) of the code you're creating. This can then be processed by various tools, to produce documentation in accessible formats like HTML and Rich Text Format.

While ServiceNow does not currently support *Intellisense* or auto-completion based on JSDoc comments, many developers build their code in a more advanced external linter/IDE such as Jetbrains' Webstorm, and JSDoc is supported in most such IDEs. Even when you're just building it in the default ServiceNow IDE though, JSDoc comments can be extremely helpful for future-you, and for other developers, to understand how to interface with your code at a glance. I strongly recommend it for **Script Includes** which may be called from within various different types of scripts.

It certainly isn't required to JSDocument every function or object in your code, but it is very strongly recommended for complex functions, especially ones in Script Includes. Here is an example of **JSDoc** usage:

```
var TimeZoneUtils = Class.create();
TimeZoneUtils.prototype = {

    /**
     * Upon initialization, you can pass in a GlideDateTime
object you've already created and set to a specific time.
     * The reference to this object will be used, and your
GDT will be modified in-place. Alternatively, you may choose
     * not to specify a parameter upon initialization, and a
new GlideDateTime object will be created, used, and returned
     * with the current time in the specified time-zone.
     *
     * @param {GlideDateTime} [gdt] - A reference to the
(optional) GlideDateTime object to be modified IN-PLACE.
     * If not specified, a new one will be generated, and a
reference returned.
     */
    initialize: function(gdt) {
            if (gdt) {
                    this.gdt = gdt;
            } else {
                    this.gdt = new GlideDateTime();
            }
    },

    /**
     * Get the GlideDateTime object (as a reference).
     * This will return a *reference* to the GlideDateTime
object. Note that because of JavaScript's
     * pass-by-reference jive, you should expect that if you
set a variable using this method, then
```

```
     * call another method which modifies the GDT object
referenced in this class, you will be modifying
     * the object to which your variable is a reference! In
other words, your variable will be modified *in-place*.
     * @returns {*|GlideDateTime}
     */
    getGDT: function() {
          return this.gdt;
    },

    /* OTHER STUFF HERE - THIS IS JUST AN EXAMPLE */

    type: 'TimeZoneUtils'
};
```

UPDATE SETS

Get your development together.

*Get your [stuff] together. Get it all together and put
it in a back pack. All your [stuff]. So it's together.*
—Morty

U PDATE SETS are used to track, maintain, and deploy your development changed – whether it's configuration, code, layouts, or anything else that's tracked in Update Sets. Once your changes are ready for deployment to another instance, Update Sets are also how you move your changes between instances. You can export them to XML (once the State is set to Complete) and import that XML into the target instance, or you can **retrieve** them from the target instance before previewing and deploying them. However you do it, it's important to *sanitize* your Update Sets, keep them clean, and keep them **functional**. That's "functional" as in "functional programming".

In this chapter, we're going to learn about **batching**, what is and **isn't** tracked in Update Sets, common pitfalls when dealing with scoped records, and how to correctly handle **preview** errors.

UPDATE SET BATCHING

ServiceNow released **Update Set batching** in the Jakarta release of the Now platform, allowing you to **group** Update Sets together in a logical hierarchical grouping. This enables you to preview and commit them in bulk, and in order.

Update Set batching takes a lot of the hassle and annoyance out of managing large groups of Update Sets for a major release, and allows you to extract a specific set of functionality from a release without impacting the rest. For example, consider a scenario where you need to do **A,** which enables you to do **B**, which enables you to then do **C**. If there's a problem with **B**, whoever does the deployment will have to be aware that **C** relies upon **B**, or the deployment of **C** will fail!

Hierarchical Update Set batching makes this process easier, but is by no means a catch-all solution. You still have to build, **maintain**, and control the Update Set hierarchy and think carefully about where each Update Set belongs in the chain.

MASTER UPDATE SETS

It's not a bad idea to begin a release or large project by creating a "Master" Update Set. This is the Update Set under which all related Update Sets will live. It's also good to have a naming convention that makes sense, but that's something your team will have to figure out internally to determine what works best. I'll use the name **Release April 2018-Master** as my example "master" Update Set.

No updates will actually go into the master Update Set. Instead, this will just be used to "contain" the Update Sets that contain any development that should be moved along as part of the "April 2018" release. Whenever a developer creates a new Update Set for some development, they'll set the **Parent** field on their Update Set to this master set.

As an example, imagine I've created two Update Sets for some development that I've been assigned stories for: **TW-Automate Inc Assignment-v1.0** and **TW-Build Catalog Item-v1.0**, and give them both helpful descriptions. I set these Update Sets' **Parent** field to **Release April 2018-Master**, since they're both scheduled for the April 2018 release, but if they needed to be pushed back at some point, I could give them a different parent. The master Update Set would not have a parent.

After identifying something additional that needs to be added, I create **TW-Build Catalog Item-v1.1**. This "1.1" Update Set will be a child of **TW-Build Catalog Item-**

v1.0 *rather than* **Release April 2018-Master**, since it is dependent directly on v1.0. This way, if the story to which they both relate needs to be moved back to the next release, I can just reassign v1.0, and v1.1 will come along with it. By making 1.1 the child of 1.0 rather than the child of the master set, I also ensure that the order of deployment is maintained, which is important because 1.1 will surely reference records contained within 1.0.

Let's have a look at what these relationships look like visually. You can click the **Visualize Update Set Batch** from any Update Set form, to see a visual representation of the relationships between your Update Sets and their hierarchy.

*Note: Right-clicking an Update Set in this view, and clicking **Prune**, will only prune it from that view. This does not actually prune the Update Set from the batch hierarchy. If you refresh the batch visualizer, the pruned Update Set will reappear.*

As you can see, from the master upset set, we split into two branches; but you can have as many child Update Sets as you like. If we then right-click on the master Update Set, and click **Edit**, we can see the **Child Update Sets** related list. This is a list of all of the Update Sets which are **immediate** children of the master set. It does not include the *children of the children* of the master set.

To see **all** of the Update Sets in the entire batch, go to the maser Update Set, and open the **Update Sets In Batch** related list.

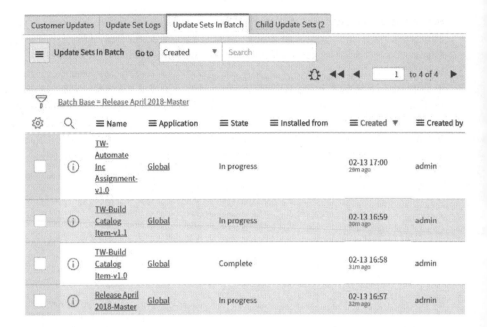

Note: *Closing the master Update Set will close **all child Update Sets in the batch**. However, closing any child Update Set – even if it has children of its own – will not close any others in the batch, including its children.*

WHAT IS AND ISN'T TRACKED

In ServiceNow, it's important to understand the difference between **data** and **configuration/customization**. Data is stuff that fills up tables

Only what ServiceNow considers **configuration/customization** is captured in Update Sets, but it can sometimes be a little bit difficult to pin down what constitutes configuration without simply knowing in advance. For this reason, if you're not 100% certain that a particular record type is indeed captured in Update Sets, it's a good idea to open your Update Set in another tab, sort your updates by the *sys_updated* column, and make sure that your changes were captured.

Records which are not "captured" in Update Sets can still be forced into them. For example, if you want to force a specific record in the **Location** [cmn_location] table (which isn't tracked) into your Update Set, you can do so in a Background

Script using the GlideUpdateManager2 API. In some cases, such as with a large number of records, it makes more sense just to export them all to XML and manually import them into the target instance after deploying your Update Set.

Pro-tip: To make it a little easier to include data records (since nearly every developer needs to do this quite often), you can download a tool I wrote, which puts a "Include in Update Set" button in the Related Links of every record and list context menu for every table that isn't tracked in Update Sets if you're an admin.
You can find this free tool at http://updatetracker.sngeek.com/!

While not exhaustive, I've provided a list of records that are included, and not included, in update sets. You might be surprised by some of the examples.

The following **are** tracked in Update Sets:
- Roles
- Form sections and layouts
- Reports
- Form and list views

The following are **not** tracked in Update Sets:
- Scheduled jobs & scheduled script executions
- Schedules
- Configuration Items
- Users
- Groups
- Group memberships
- Role assignment (to users *or* groups)
- Homepages/Dashboards

You'll also find that there are certain records that are dependent on other records for their functionality. For example, if you create a role in the **Role** [sys_user_role] table, that will be tracked. If you then create a **group** (which isn't tracked), add the **role** to that group, and then force that group into your update set, you might be surprised to find that the roles you gave it **didn't come along with it**. This is because the associations between roles and groups is stored in the **sys_group_has_role** table which is also not tracked in update sets. Similarly, the association between **users** and roles is in the **sys_user_has_role** table, which is also not tracked in update sets.

There is a similar situation that happens with **dashboards**. Dashboards contain several linked *pieces* that are each not captured in update sets. Each new tab in the

71

pa_tabs table is linked to two tables (**sys_portal_page** and **sys_grid_canvas**). To get dashboards into your update set, you have to grab each of those types of records.

TRACKING SCOPED RECORDS

To be honest, working with Update Sets inside of scoped applications in ServiceNow can be a real bother. In this section, we'll go over a few specific rules to be aware of.

For starters, it's important to understand that a single Update Set should never contain records from multiple application scopes. The platform tries to prevent this, but for some reason, it happens anyway. If at all possible, you want to avoid it at all costs. Update Sets have a specific scope, and you cannot deploy updates in one scope using an Update Set in another scope.

There are plenty of scenarios where you may need to work within multiple scopes. For example, the **HR** application consists of multiple separate application scopes including **Human Resources: Core** and **Human Resources: Service Portal**. One development effort may require that you work with records in both HR scopes, as well as records in the Global scope. This typically requires manually creating **three separate Update Sets**: one for each scope. The Update Set you have selected persists when you switch back to a specific scope, but not between scopes.

For example, if you have **Update Set 1** selected in the **Human Resources: Core** scope, then you switch to the **Global** scope and select **Update Set 2**, and finally switch *back* to the **Human Resources: Core** scope, you'll find that you still have **Update Set 1** selected. This will persist until you change your Update Set *while in that scope*.

There are some additional headaches to contend with, too. For example: typically, when you visit a record that's in a different scope than your session is in, you cannot edit the record and you get a warning like this:

> ⓘ This record is in the Human Resources: Core application, but Global is the current application. To edit this record click here.

You can click the link at the end of that message to switch (for the duration of one update) to the scope in which the record resides, but you won't be able to see what Update Set is selected in that scope unless you switch your whole session to the relevant scope.

Another reason to be very careful when dealing with scoped updates, is that some **tables** are in a certain scope, but the **records** in them are in a different scope. Again, ServiceNow is working on this, but when this happens, there is no good way to tell that you're effectively poisoning your Update Set with updates in multiple scopes, making it so it won't be able to be deployed.

For an example of this, consider the following steps:

1. Select the **Human Resources: Core** application
2. Create an Update Set in the **Human Resources: Core** application. Set it as your current Update Set.
3. Navigate to the **sn_hr_core_service** table.
4. Open any record in that table, and make any update to it, so the record is captured in your Update Set.

You'll notice that the record is tracked in your Update Set. However, in some instances, you'll also notice that even though the **sn_hr_core_service** table (like your Update Set) is in the **Human Resources: Core** scope, the update itself is in the **Global** scope. This Update Set cannot be deployed until all updates it contains are in the same scope that it's in.

Unfortunately, the only way around this right now when dealing with multiple scopes, is to double-check that any new updates you make are tracked in your Update Set, and in the correct scope.

Note: ServiceNow has been making an effort to patch this issue wherever they find it by updating the plugin, but they do not usually offer retroactive patches if you've already deployed a given scoped application or plugin. You might have some luck if you notice this issue in your instance, by opening a HI ticket (http://hi.servicenow.com/). The key is just to keep an eye on it to make sure your Update Set and update scopes match.

PERFORMANCE

Taking it to eleven

Time dilation occurs at relativistic speeds as well as in the presence of intense gravitational fields, and while waiting for a webpage to load.
—*This chapter quote*

I'm So Meta, Even This Acronym
—*I.S.M.E.T.A.*

PERFORMANCE IS IMPORTANT. Whether it comes in the form of query efficiency, database table configuration, or default layouts, building something that people are going to enjoy using, means building something that's **fast**.

It's tempting to include all the features and fields and really fancy logic and queries to add a bit of chrome to your application or solution, but every business knows that the **value** of everything should be considered in the context of its **cost**. Every person-hour spent waiting for a page to load or for a query to complete has a financial cost, as well as a cost that can be most effectively measured in Average-Rage-Per-Human, or ARPH. You want to keep your ARPH low, and your efficiency high.

QUERY EFFICIENCY

It's important to be **efficient** when querying the database (which includes GlideRecord queries). To that end, this section contains some basic guidelines for making sure your queries are efficient.

Inefficient database operations can be the source

SINGLE-RECORD QUERIES

Any time you use an `if` block rather than a loop (such as `if (gr.next()) {}` rather than `while (gr.next()) {}`), that means you're only querying for **one** record. The most efficient way to do this is to use the GlideRecord `.get()` API, and pass in a single argument: a **sys_id** or an **encoded query**. If it is not possible to specify a sys_id, then use `gr.setLimit(1)` to tell the database to stop searching after the first record is found. Otherwise, this would be like continuing to search for your keys, after you've found them; which is why they're always in the *last* place you look. By the same token, if you are only expecting (or if you only *want*) a certain maximum number of records to be found, be sure to use `.setLimit()` to make the query easier on the database, and improve performance.

NESTED QUERIES

It's also a good idea to avoid using **nested queries** if it can be at all avoided, as explained in the **Iterators** section of the **Naming Conventions** chapter. This is because nested queries usually require a separate "inner" query for every single loop of the "outer" query, and can almost always be written more efficiently.

Make your queries as efficient (and **specific**) as possible. For example, if you only do something with the records returned from your query in the event that a specific condition is true, then that condition should be **part of the query**! Consider the following code:

```
var grIncident = new GlideRecord('incident');
grIncident.addActiveQuery();
```

```
grIncident.query();
while (grIncident.next()) {
    if (grIncident.getValue('state') === '3') {
    gs.print('Incident ' + grIncident.getValue('number') + '
is in state: 3.');
    }
}
```

In this example, our database query would be monumentally more efficient if we were to add the condition currently in the `if` block, to the query itself, like so:

```
var grIncident = new GlideRecord('incident');
grIncident.addActiveQuery();
grIncident.addQuery('state', '3');
grIncident.query();
while (grIncident.next()) {
    gs.print('Incident ' + grIncident.getValue('number') + '
is in state 3.');
}
```

There; that's **much** better!

QUERY ORDER

It's important to realize – especially when dealing with very large or poorly optimized tables – that the **order** of your queries matters. I'm not talking about the GlideRecord `.orderBy()` method; I'm talking about the order in which you add your query filters.

*Note: The instance **caches** the results of a query for extremely quick subsequent retrieval, and once cached, the order of query parameters is much less important. However, it's still important to write our queries for **maximum efficiency**!*

According to a community post by one of our contributors, JarodM, you can reduce your query time by up to or even over **90%** on the first query after instance cache is cleared by following a few simple steps to ensure your queries are ordered properly.

You can see the post we're referring to at http://performancepost.sngeek.com/.

To understand why your query order matters, consider the following scenario:

Say you have 1,000 records in the Incident table: 900 **inactive** records, and 100 **active** records. Imagine you'd like to get all **active** Incidents where the **Short description** field contains the phrase "oh god, why is this happening".

The work of checking whether the **active** field is **true** is really quite easy, but the work of checking whether a string **contains** another string can be (comparatively speaking) much more costly. For that reason, in the above scenario, it would make sense to put the **active** query **first** and the **contains** query **second**. The reason that this is more performance-friendly, is that the first query – being **less computationally intensive** – filters out 90% of the records that you have to do the *more* computationally intensive **contains** query on.

Pro-tip. There is a quick-and-easy <u>server-side</u> GlideRecord API for adding an active query. Rather than writing `gr.addQuery('active',` `'true')`*, you can use the simpler* `gr.addActiveQuery()`*. There does not appear to be any performance benefit to this, however.*

To simplify this into a general rule: Always try to put the **less computationally intensive** query filters **first**, so you have to do the more intensive operations on fewer records to filter your results.

TABLES & LISTS

In another chapter of this compendium, we learned about the importance of adding unnecessarily large fields to a database table (especially a base table like **Task** [task]), but consider that it's also costly in terms of performance, to add such long fields to a form or list view. Even if these fields are **hidden** on the form, their contents **must still be retrieved** from the server and sent to the client. For especially long fields, this can have a noticeable impact on the form's load-time. For this reason, it's a good idea to avoid putting fields on the form if they don't need to be there; and the same goes for lists.

Another thing to consider, is how your lists are **ordered**. Ordering a large list by a field that isn't **indexed** can have significant performance impacts. This performance cost is even greater for fields that have a higher computational cost to order, such as a non-indexed **date/time** field.

*Pro-tip. Many users complain about how slow ServiceNow is when they first log in, but you'll often notice that these long transactions are caused by them loading their **homepage**.*

A homepage can consist of widget-after-widget containing large, poorly-optimized lists with poorly optimized queries, data visualizations, and so on. It might be a good idea to enable a default **blank** homepage user preference in the **sys_user_preference** table.

CONCLUSION

Did you get the memo?

Wow, I learned so much. This book was great. In fact, I'm going to go rate it 5-stars on every website ever!
—You, probably

I n this developer compendium, we have aimed to provide tips, tricks, guidelines, best-practices, and standards that can be applied in any environment with a positive result. If you're an architect or code reviewer, we hope that you'll have found some best-practices here that you can apply to your instance, and that you might consider distributing this book to your developers in order to improve the quality and time-to-production of their solutions. If you're a developer or administrator, we hope you'll keep this book around to refer back to and reference whenever you're not sure how to handle a situation we discussed in these pages.

We also hope that whether you're a new developer or a greybeard and senior architect, you feel like you've learned something from this developer's compendium. For free ServiceNow tools and more educational ServiceNow developer-oriented content, check out our website and blog over at http://sngeek.com/.

If you feel like we've missed anything, got anything wrong, or if you have some tips or guidelines you'd like to contribute, please email Tim@SNGeek.com. Any tips you contribute may end up in the next edition, and if you're the first person to point it out, you'll be credited as a contributor in the beginning of this book. You are also welcome to contact us using that email address if you have any questions, or if your company is looking for some ServiceNow architectural or development support!

Finally, thank you – dear reader – for buying this little developer's handbook. If you are so inclined, I humbly welcome you to leave a review on Amazon, GoodReads, or wherever else is convenient. I also welcome you to check out some of my other books, over at http://books.sngeek.com/.

Made in the USA
San Bernardino, CA
11 July 2018